Fathers

They're the guys who get to light short-fuse Roman candles on July Fourth and cart sixteen-foot evergreens on Christmas Eve. The men whose best sweaters end up as blankets for the family dog. Valiant, dedicated souls willing to hike, roller skate, and even take up plumbing for the women and children they love. D.L. Stewart has lived it, and now, much to his family's distress, describes it all.

"WRY AND WITTY . . . like most good humor writing, these tales have more than just a nugget of truth and everyone who has ever lived with wife or child will find this book a delight."
—*Chattanooga Times*

"Stewart is to family men what Erma Bombeck is to family women—she the Socrates of the ironing board, he Solomon of the gray flannel suit set. . . . Stewart's wit spills over."
—*Cincinnati Enquirer*

"Until Stewart came along no one was speaking for today's American father."   —*Columbus Dispatch*

"Stewart proves that one can be a father and still retain a sense of humor—perhaps in self-defense."   —*Seattle Times*

"Every chapter of *Fathers Are People Too* is humorous, satirical, feisty and fun to identify with. Hilarious but oh-so-true. . . . If the kids are getting you down (or, kids, if your parents are getting you down) try living with the Stewarts for 17 terrifically joyous chapters."   —*Fresno Bee*

Also by D.L. Stewart
Father Knows Best—Sometimes

About the Author

D.L. Stewart is the author of Father Knows Best—Sometimes!
He and his wive have coauthored four children, and they all
live in Beavercreek, Ohio, along with a constantly
disassembling automobile, an impossible-to-assemble
barbecue grill, and a Frisbee-eating dog. In addition to his
books and syndicated writings, Stewart has published arti-
cles in Good Housekeeping, McCall's, and Redbook. He has
also been a guest on such television programs as Hour Magazine and The Merv Griffin Show.

Fathers Are People Too

D. L. Stewart

Illustrations by Ted Pitts

WARNER BOOKS

A Warner Communications Company

Warner Books Edition
Copyright © 1980, 1983 by the McNaught Syndicate, Inc.
All rights reserved.

This Warner Books edition is published by arrangement with
the Bobbs-Merrill Co., Inc., 630 Third Avenue, New York, New York 10017

Warner Books, Inc., 666 Fifth Avenue, New York, NY 10103

W A Warner Communications Company

Printed in the United States of America
First Warner Books Printing: June 1986
10 9 8 7 6 5 4 3 2

This is a revised edition of *Fathers Are People Too* which was
previously published in 1980 by the Journal Herald, Dayton, Ohio.

Library of Congress Cataloging-in-Publication Data

Stewart, D. L., 1942–
    Fathers are people too.

    Reprint. Previously published: Indianapolis :
Bobbs-Merrill, c1983.
    1. Stewart, D. L., 1942–   2. Fathers—Ohio—
Biography.   I. Title.
[HQ756.S818   1986]   306.8'742   85-26621
ISBN 0-446-37000-2 (U.S.A.) (pbk.)
      0-446-37005-3 (Canada) (pbk.)

To my two beautiful children
. . . also the other two

Contents

Foreword

What's it like being the children of a famous newspaper columnist?

We really wouldn't know.

But even being the kids of a semi-well-liked, small-town writer has its annoying, as well as its rewarding, moments.

Sometimes we all wish that we could take him on our yearly trip to Kings Island amusement park and lose him for the summer on the Beast. But most of the time we really like the feeling of going places with a face that people recognize. Once you learn to dodge the rotten tomatoes and wadded up newspapers, it can really be fun.

About the only difference we can see between having a celebrity and, say, a plumber for a father is that we have been exposed to an awful lot more strange people and the even stranger things that they do.

Like, how many middle-class, suburban kids have double-dated with their fathers on prom night? Or eaten hippo-burger for dinner? Or had every thing they've done, said or thought mentioned in the newspaper?

On second thought, you probably get more out of having a plumber for a father. At least your faucets don't leak.

Nope, being D. L. Stewart's kids is not the easiest job in the world.

But it's a living.

—LAURIE, MIKE, ERIC and JAMIE STEWART

Fathers Are People Too

1

Two is enough

When we got married, I knew she wanted to have children. But I didn't know she was going to be a fanatic about it.

My idea of a family is a little boy with freckles, a little girl with pigtails and a Jaguar XKE with a stereo tape deck. Her idea of a family is the Mormon Tabernacle Choir.

Before we are married, we spend a great deal of time discussing this issue.

"I definitely don't want to have just one," she says. "Being an only child is tough."

Having grown up as an only child, I have to agree with her. When you're an only child, you don't have anybody to give your strep throat to. When you're an only child, you have to drive the babysitter crazy all by yourself. Worst of all, when you're an only child, you never have anybody to blame. When I was 14 my father came into my room and asked me who had been smoking his cigarettes. I had to tell him it was the dog.

"We probably should have two kids," I say. "Especially if one is a boy and the other is a girl. The way I look at it, that would pretty much exhaust the possibilities."

"I was thinking we should have four," she says.

"Four? No way. We are absolutely not going to have that many kids. Two for sure. Three maybe. But definitely not four. And that's final. As we stroll down life's path together, you will discover that once I have made up my mind, I will never change it. So you can just forget about having four kids. That's my last word on the subject."

★ ★ ★

The first of our four kids is born nine months and two hours after we are married. It is a beautiful baby, with the broad shoulders of a linebacker. The thick legs of a shot-putter. The huge hands of a basketball player.

I rush from the nursery to the new mother's bed. "Did you see the baby?" she asks, sleepily.

"I sure did."

"Are you happy?"

"Am I happy? What father wouldn't be happy with a kid like that?"

"Have you settled on a name?"

"I think we should call her Laurie."

Becoming a father is easy. Fun, even. Figuring out what to do with the by-product is a whole different story. When you are 21 years old and you have a wife and baby, a certain feeling comes over you. Sometimes it is a warm feeling. That's usually when you're holding the baby on your lap.

More often, the feeling is of inadequacy. The thing is, there is no training to be a father. In high school, they teach you how to find the square root of pi, but they don't teach you how to find the key to the bathroom when your wife is at the store and your three-year-old is locked inside. With the water running. Under the door.

In college, they teach you to put together a term paper on the history of 18th Century journalism in Great Britain. But nobody thinks to teach you how to put together a 10-speed bike while your 12-year-old sits there watching with excitement on his face and faith in his heart.

To make matters worse, kids are not necessarily like the ones you see on the *Brady Bunch*.

When our first-born is three, for instance, we take her to the circus. It is our first opportunity to see her little eyes sparkle and hear her happy squeals of laughter under the big top. So we lay out money for tickets. We lay out money for program/coloring books. For balloons. For cotton candy. For a push button, glow-in-the-dark baton that everybody is supposed to wave when the ringmaster gives the signal. By the time the circus begins, there is nothing left to buy. Even if there was, we couldn't afford it unless we found a vendor who took Master Charge.

It is a terrific circus. The clowns clown around. The acrobats acrobat around. The horses horse around. Through it all, the three-year-old sits there like a lump. She has more fun than this when we have beets for dinner.

Just as we are about to give it all up, she jumps up in her seat.

"Look there, look there," she shouts, pointing towards the elephants. Well, not exactly towards the elephants. Actually, where she is pointing is just a little bit behind the elephants. For the first time that evening, her eyes sparkle and her laughter comes in happy squeals.

Unaware of the pleasure he is bringing, the man behind the elephants continues to do his broom and dustpan routine.

It is a few years later. A different kid. We take him to the country to see some moo-cows and some horseys. We stop by a fence and a horsey obligingly trots over to us. The kid is thrilled. I am thrilled. The horse is not necessarily thrilled, but he is being a good sport about it.

The kid giggles and smiles. I focus my camera. The kid reaches out his small hand. I poise my camera. The kid ignores the horse and pets the fence.

Yet another in what is starting to look like an inexhaustible supply of kids. He is sitting on the couch with his grandmother, who is reading to him from the big picture book. *T'was the Night Before Christmas.* It is a warm and lovely scene. Norman Rockwell would've hocked his pipe to paint it.

Grandma is at the part where Santa has fulfilled his obligations and is preparing to whisk back up the chimney by means of laying his finger aside of his nose. A full-page picture illustrates this rather noteworthy achievement.

The kid looks at the picture. He looks at his grandmother. His eyes grow wide with wonder.

"Grandma?" he asks in a small, soft voice. "How come Santa is picking his nose?"

How deep
is my toilet?

There is some disagreement as to when a man actually becomes a father. Many feel that it happens at the moment of conception. Others argue that it is not until the actual moment of birth.

I always sort of figured that a man is not really a father until he has pulled his first Lincoln Log out of the toilet bowl.

You can tell a veteran father from a rookie a mile away. A veteran father is the one who always walks around with one sleeve rolled up. The one with the Sani-Flush stains on his forearm. Fatherhood came to me on the day our first-born got her first set of crayons. Since then, I have fished out several thousand crayons, two pounds of marbles, four generations of Fisher-Price people and a turtle named Fred. I am not quite sure how Fred got there. But I am told that he was trying to commit suicide.

The big test of fatherhood, however, does not come until she is seven years old and knocks in her first comb. As she watches it disappear in a swirl of bright blue water, she does what any other seven-year-old would do in a similar situation. She calls for someone else to come and get it out.

"Why can't she get it out herself?" I ask the woman who promised to love, honor and explain life's mysteries to me.

"She says her arm's too short."

"Is this the same seven-year-old who can reach the entire length of a formal dining room table to snatch the last cookie off the plate before her brother can get to it?"

"How do I know? What's the difference? Just stick your hand down in the nice clear, cool water and get it out."

"Wait a minute. Why do I have to get the comb out? Why can't you stick your hand down in the nice clear, cool water and get it out?"

"Put my hand in there? You must be kidding. Besides, your sleeve is already rolled up."

"Oh, all right."

I stick my hand into the nice clear, cool water. Slowly I work my fingers around the bend at the bottom. Painstakingly I slide my hand deeper into the pipe. Aha! I can feel something with my fingertips. Aha! It is not the comb.

I wash my fingertips and go to the garage for the plunger. Returning to the bathroom, I plunge back into the battle. After five minutes of plunging, all the water that was in the bowl is on the floor. And all the combs that were stuck in the pipe are still stuck in the pipe.

"I think we need a snake," I say.

"I think we need a plumber," she says.

"Are you kidding? Do you have any idea how much a plumber charges?"

"Not that much. I read an ad in the paper the other day for a plumber who only charges $5 an hour."

"Sure. But he doesn't make house calls."

From a neighbor, I borrow a plumber's snake, which is a long S-shaped spring. I use it for several minutes without success. Apparently the snake is defective. No matter how hard I hit the toilet with it, the comb refuses to come out.

A short time later the snake's owner comes over. I mention to him about the defective snake. He explains to me that you do not hit the toilet with it. You carefully twist it into the pipe, dislodging whatever foreign material might be stuck in there.

He carefully twists it into the pipe, dislodging whatever foreign material might be stuck in there. But he does not budge that comb.

"I think you're going to have to get it from underneath," he says, finally, taking me down to the basement and showing me where the pipe is that I will have to disconnect. I look up at the pipe. I'm not sure what will come out of it if I disconnect it. And I'm pretty sure I don't want to find out.

I thank the neighbor with the snake. I go back upstairs. I call a plumber. A veteran father would never do that. But a smart father would.

Of course, you can't call a plumber for every little chore. So when the woman who promised to love, honor and jiggle my handle comes home from the store one day with a new toilet seat, I know that I'm probably going to be on my own this time. I know that if it's going to be fixed, I'm going to have to fix it. What I don't know is why.

Or, as I point out to her:

"What do we need a new toilet seat for? We still have the old one."

"I know, but it's yellow."

"With three boys, that's probably just as well."

"But the towels and the wash clothes and the soap all are blue."

"So?"

"What do you mean, 'so?' It makes the bathroom look terrible. What will people think?"

I run that through my mind for awhile. What WILL people think when they discover that we have a bathroom with a yellow toilet seat and blue soap? What will the neighbors think? What will our friends think? What will my employers think?

"DL, I'm afraid we're going to have to let you go . . . Your work? No, that's not it. Your work is no worse than it ever was. It's just that, well, we try not to interfere in our employees' lives, but some things can't be overlooked. And if word gets around that you have a yellow toilet seat and blue soap in the same bathroom, well, I'm sure you can see what that might lead to . . . I knew you'd understand. After all, I've got the welfare of an entire company to think about."

And, even if I can take it, what about the kids?

"Hello, Mr. Stewart? This is the school nurse calling . . . No, no, there's nothing to be alarmed about. Your seven-year-old just got into a little scrape with some of the other children on the playground. I'm sure she'll be fine after the transfusions. I don't know if she's told you, Mr. Stewart, but she's been getting into quite a few of these scrapes lately. The other children have been tormenting her mercilessly ever since they found out that you have a yellow toilet seat and blue soap in the same bathroom. And, frankly Mr. Stewart, I don't blame them."

I dig out my tool box and go to work on the toilet seat.

Although I have had little formal training in toilet seat changing, it seems only logical to me that the first step most likely would be to remove the old toilet seat.

Removing an old toilet seat is a simple operation, requiring only a socket wrench, a screwdriver, a pair of pliers and a pound and a half of nitroglycerine. This is because the toilet seat is fastened to the toilet with two bolts that are rusted to two nuts. That can only be reached from underneath. By someone whose fingers are 23 inches long.

Not having a socket wrench, nitroglycerine or 23-inch fingers, I spend the next hour and a half on my back with a pair of pliers and a steak knife.

Eventually I remove one rusted bolt. But the other one is not so easy. That's because it's located on the other side of the toilet, the side that is very close to the wall. You could almost say that the toilet is flush to the wall. There is not enough room for me to get my body in there. There is not enough room to get Twiggy's body in there.

But, through imaginative rearrangement of my exterior limbs, I finally work my way under the sink and into the space between the toilet and the wall. I work quickly. Or, as quickly as it's possible to work when you are wedged between a toilet and a hard place, with one arm underneath you, one leg wrapped around the bowl, the other resting on top of the Charmin and your face pressed against a pipe that is cold. And leaking. I feel something like Michelangelo. But he was lucky. He only had to do ceilings.

All told, it takes four hours, a broken steak knife, a cut finger and a backache that has me walking like Quasimodo to replace the old yellow toilet seat with the new blue one. But it is worth it to keep our bathroom from being the laughingstock of the entire town.

Besides, it's good training for the day she decides to redecorate an entire room. Not that she actually tells me that she has decided to redecorate an entire room, of course. It just sort of happens.

I am dozing in my comfortable old orange recliner dreaming my favorite dream, the one where Sophia Loren is listing in alphabetical order the reasons why she prefers middle-aged newspaper columnists. She has just passed G and is heading for H. Slowly, a soft smile on her lips, she comes closer. This one always embarrasses her a little, so she likes to whisper it in my ear. Her hair brushes across my cheek, her breath is warm on my neck, her voice is husky as she says:

"How about if we get a red wastebasket for this room and put the green one in the five-year-old's room?"

That's not Sophia Loren's voice. It is the voice of the woman who promised to love, honor and never wake me when I'm smiling.

"Huh? What did you say, dear?"

"I said, how about if we get a red wastebasket for this room and put the green one in the five-year-old's room? I saw one at Bargain City for $3.98."

"Whatever you say, dear." I am nothing if not agreeable. Besides, this is no time for long discussions. Sophia gets so lonely when I'm gone.

When I come home from work the next day, there is a new red wastebasket in the family room. I notice it right away, because it is sitting next to where my comfortable old orange recliner used to be.

"What happened to my chair?"

"It's in the bedroom," she says.

"Why?"

"Because it just didn't look good with the new red wastebasket."

"But that's my television-watching chair. Do you have any idea of how hard it's going to be to sit in a chair that's on the second floor and watch a television that's on the first floor?"

"Don't worry. I've ordered a new recliner. It should be here tomorrow."

The next day a new recliner arrives. It is dark brown vinyl. The kind that sticks to the backs of your legs in summer and sends a chill up your spine in winter.

"You'll love it," she says. "And it's going to look terrific next to the new drapes."

"New drapes?"

"Of course. You didn't think I was going to spend all that money on a new chair and then have it sit next to some ratty old drapes?"

"I must have been crazy."

Two days later the new drapes arrive.

"I suppose you want me to hang them tonight," I say.

"No. There's no sense hanging them before you do the painting."

"What painting?"

"The painting you're going to do on the walls. You didn't think I was going to spend all that money on new drapes and then hang them against those dingy-looking walls?"

"So what color is the paint?"

"Gray."

That evening, as I am brightening up the dingy walls with the gray paint, she says:

"Boy, I didn't realize you were such a sloppy painter. It's a good thing the new couch hasn't arrived yet."

"New couch?"

"Of course. You didn't think . . ."

"I know, I know. Only, I'm going to be really glad when you run out of things to buy. You've replaced everything in the room but the window. So far, this red wastebasket has cost me two months' salary."

"Don't worry," she says, "as soon as the credenza comes in, we'll be finished."

"What do we need with a credenza? Nobody in our family knows how to play one."

"You don't play them. You put things in them. We're going to use ours as a liquor cabinet."

"But we never drink liquor. Only beer and Kool-Aid."

"We could serve it to our friends."

"We don't have any friends."

"If we had liquor to serve to them, we might."

Eventually the drapes are up, the couch is in, the walls are gray and we own a credenza to hold the liquor we never buy to serve to friends we don't have.

"I assume you're satisfied now?" I say, as we sit in our redecorated room.

"It's just perfect," she says. "Except for that red wastebasket."

3
Every dad
needs a dog

In the first eight years of our domestic bliss, we accumulate two kids, a three-bedroom house in the suburbs, two cars, a quarter-acre of immortal crabgrass and enough debts to sink General Motors.

The only thing missing is a pet.

I suggest to the woman who promised to love, honor and cook my Alpo that it's time the kids had a puppy. Every kid, I point out, should have a dog. There's probably a federal law against kids who don't have dogs. She is not entirely convinced. I can tell she is not entirely convinced by the look on her face as she thumbs through the Yellow Pages until she gets to "Lawyers, divorce."

"Every family in this neighborhood has a dog," I say.

"Sure," she says, "and they all come into our yard to do their dirty work. Why should we get one too?"

"To get even."

"Well, you may have a point there. But if we do get a dog, it has to be just the right kind."

She describes exactly what kind of dog she will tolerate and the next day we visit the Animal Shelter in search of a dog that doesn't bark, doesn't shed, catches its own food, won't go to the bathroom within five miles of our yard and can be trained for baby-sitting and light housekeeping.

At the Animal Shelter, we go from cage to cage as she examines and rejects one dog after another. Too big. Too small. Too noisy. Too awake.

"Too awake?"

"Right," she says. "Besides not barking or having long hair, I want one that sleeps a lot."

"You don't want a dog, you want a sloth."

Finally, at the end of the row, she spots a little white puppy with one brown ear, trembling in the back of a cage. It looks like the RCA Victor dog in the middle of a nervous breakdown.

"This is the one," she says, dragging the puppy out of its cage and carrying it to the front desk. At the front desk we pay $8 and receive the proper papers to identify us as the owners of this noble animal. According to the papers, our dog does not have impressive bloodlines. Its mother, on the other hand, did have an impressive number of canine acquaintances. All of them male.

As we are about to walk out the door, I ask the lady at the front desk how old she thinks he is.

"He?"

"Sure. He. The dog we just bought."

"I don't mean to be disrespectful, sir," she says, "but whoever taught you biology must have been real new at it."

"You mean . . ."

"I mean SHE is about eight weeks old."

It proves to be a $75 misunderstanding, which is what it costs us to make sure that there will never be a bunch of little nervous RCA Victor dogs running around our house.

We name her April. As in April Fool. Quickly, she becomes a part of our family. Just how big a part I discover the next year when I come home and see the nine-year-old getting out the good tablecloth and the silverware that makes all our food taste like silver polish.

"We having company?" I ask.

"It's a birthday party," she says. This puzzles me, because I am not aware of any impending birthdays in our family. And I take particular pride in knowing the birthdates in my family. The nine-year-old's is during the Indianapolis 500. The six-year-old's is during the Master's golf tournament. Their mother's is during the World Series.

"It can't be anybody's birthday," I protest. "This is still basketball season."

"It is, too," she says. "It's April's."

"But, April's a dog. Dogs don't have birthday parties. What makes you think I'm going to go along with having a birthday party for a dog?"

"If we don't have a party for her," the nine-year-old says, "she'll probably die of a broken heart. Then you'll have to bury her, which means trying to dig a hole in the frozen ground and you'll probably throw your back out again and you won't be able to go to work and you'll lose your job so you won't be able to keep up the house payments and . . ."

"All right, all right, have the party." The nine-year-old gets more like her mother every day.

Preparations for the birthday party resume. In addition to the tablecloth and silverware, decorations are strung throughout the dining room and a large sign that says "Happy Birthday April" is taped across the hutch. From various hiding places appear a bevy of gift-wrapped presents, party hats and a birthday cake baked in the shape of a fox terrier.

"I didn't know they made cake pans shaped like fox terriers," I admit to the nine-year-old. "They don't," she says, "I've got this book that shows you how to make cakes in different shapes. See, you can make a dog, a butterfly, a teddy bear, a snowman, a turtle or a lion."

"Oh," I say, temporarily rendered speechless by the thought that anyone could eat a cake shaped like a turtle. Anyway, this whole birthday thing is starting to depress me. On my last birthday, they stuck two candles in the lemon-lime Jell-O and gave me a quick chorus of "Happy Birthday, Dear Whatshisname."

But it is too late to call off the party now. April is already wearing her party hat.

With an air of anticipation, dinner is finished quickly and then it is time for the party. The presents and the cake shaped like a fox terrier are brought in. An extra chair is drawn up to the table so that April can hop up and see what's happening as I light the candles on top of the cake.

Which is when it occurs to me that this whole thing is getting out of hand. The mutt that we paid $8 for at the Animal Shelter is sitting on a chair in the dining room, with a pink party hat on her head and her paws on the table, eyeing the leftover chicken. And me, like a dummy, I'm lighting candles and singing "Happy Birthday, Dear April" to her.

Before I am able to arrive at a logical reason for all of this, the song has ended and her presents are being given to her. The nine-year-old gives her a chewy bone. The six-year-old gives her a bowl with a picture of Snoopy dining at Antoine's on the bottom. The woman who promised to love, honor and hold my leash gives her a hair brush that mysteriously disappeared from my dresser drawer three days ago.

"How come you're giving the dog my hair brush?" I ask her.

"We didn't think she'd like your hot comb. Besides, you didn't give her anything."

"I thought I'd just give her money and let her go buy whatever she wanted."

Defeated, I retreat to the family room. If there is any consolation in this whole miserable business, it is that the nine-year-old has agreed to bake a cake for me on my next birthday. And I've already decided what kind I want. It will be a chocolate fudge marble cake. Baked in the shape of Sophia Loren.

Although it is obvious that she is loved at our house, April does not become a big favorite in the neighborhood. In terms of popularity, you would have to consider her the canine equivalent of Richard Nixon. She is the only dog I ever heard of who gets threatening phone calls.

Mostly this is because she is very protective of what she considers "her" territory. "Her" territory, as nearly as we can tell, is an area bounded on the east by the Allegheny Mountains and on the west by the Colorado River. She will bark furiously at anyone who jogs through it, bikes around it or flies over it.

Her main targets are other dogs, but she also carries on a constant war with teenage boys, whom she is able to distinguish from teenage girls at distances of up to 150 yards. This is, apparently, a special sense nature gives only to dogs.

On the day she comes home bruised and bleeding, with her tail between her legs, it is obvious that she has reached what can only be considered a low point in her neighborhood relations.

I inspect her wounds. By their number, it is clear that she barks better than she fights.

"What happened to her," asks the woman who promised to love, honor and clean my kennel.

"She's been bitten by another dog."

"Are you sure it was a dog?"

"Of course I'm sure. At this hour all the teenage boys are in school. And whoever did it really cleaned her clock."

"What do you think we should do about it?"

"Well, we could enroll her in karate school."

"I mean about her wounds."

"Oh, I'm sure that if we leave her alone, she'll be all right. They really aren't that deep. Besides, nature knows how to take care of these things."

That evening, when I come home from work, I find the dog sleeping on my recliner in front of the television. Which might not bother me if it isn't for the fact that she is wearing the new brown sweater I got for Christmas.

I should, I suppose, be thankful that she is not also wearing my slippers and sipping my Chablis. Still, I am hard pressed to keep a certain note of irritation out of my voice as I inquire:

"Why the heck is that stupid mangy dog wearing my new brown sweater?"

"Because your old blue one is dirty," answers a familiar voice from the kitchen.

"What I mean is, why is she wearing a sweater at all?"

"Because she's been shivering all day long. I called the vet and he said we should keep her warm until she feels better."

Even after she is served her dinner, a great deal of which winds up on the front of my new brown sweater, the dog does not move from my recliner in front of the television. That evening I sit on the floor to watch television.

"Well, " I say, after the 11o'clock news "I think I'll go to bed now."

"Wait a minute," says the woman who promised to love, honor and tuck me in, "what about the dog?"

"It looks to me like she's planning on staying up for Johnny Carson."

"I don't mean that. I mean, she hasn't been outside all day long."

"So, send her out."

"It hurts her too much to walk. You'll have to carry her out."

"Are you nuts? I'm not going to carry any stupid, mangy dog outside in the middle of the night. If she really has to go outside, she'll get up and go."

"Suit yourself. It's your sweater."

I carry the stupid, mangy dog outside. In the dark. In the snow. With the temperature at about 100 degrees below numb. The dog looks at me. She looks at the snow. She hobbles back inside.

That routine lasts for about a week. A week of her wearing my new brown sweater. A week of her sleeping in my recliner. A week of unproductive trips outside in the middle of the night.

Eventually her wounds heal and she is able to drag herself out of my recliner and walk outside again like a normal dog. Fortunately, she has not been attacked again. I knew those karate lessons would pay off.

But that really isn't the end of the problem because, to make sure the infection doesn't return, she has to take pills for a while. One of the mysteries of dog ownership is why will a mutt who inhales an entire can of dog food before the bowl reaches the floor refuse to swallow one little pill?

The problem is brought to my attention a few days later by the woman who promised to love, honor and scratch behind my ears.

"The dog won't take her pill," she reports.

"Well, I wouldn't force her," I point out, "it may be a religious matter with her."

"It's not THAT kind of pill. They're for her infection. She has to take one every morning and every evening."

"So, what do you want me to do?"

"Talk to her."

"Talk to her? She's a dog, for crying out loud."

"OK, don't talk to her. The worst that can happen is that the infection will get worse, and we'll have to rush her to the vet's in the middle of the night, and he'll give her a whole bunch of expensive shots that won't be covered by your group medical plan, and she'll get so weak again that you'll have to carry her when she needs to go outside and stand with her while she . . ."

There is, I am sure, a great deal more to this speech, but I do not hear it. I am on my way to the kitchen to talk with the dog.

I find her sleeping in front of the refrigerator.

"Uh, excuse me, we need to have a little talk," I begin.

She opens one eye to see who it is. She looks up at me, her master, the lord of the house, king of the castle and ruler of this entire domain. She closes her eye and goes back to sleep.

"Wake up," I shout. "You're taking this pill, and that's all there is to it. I'm not fooling around with you." Sometimes a king has to be tough.

She wakes up. She looks at the bright orange pill I have placed on the floor in front of her. She sniffs it. She opens her mouth. She yawns. She goes back to sleep. I am starting to feel a little like Louis XVI just before the Revolution.

Obviously, some deception is called for here. She is, after all, a mere dog. And not a very smart one, at that. How hard can it be? I simply will fool her into playing her favorite game, the one where I toss a scrap of food into the air and she catches it and swallows it in one gulp. She does that with anything you throw her: a piece of popcorn, a dog biscuit, a side of beef.

I toss the pill up into the air. She catches it in her mouth, just as she always does. This time, however, she throws it back.

I toss the pill again. She throws it back again. For the next ten minutes we have a lively game of catch in the kitchen. She catches the pill every time. She throws it back every time. It's starting to look like spring training in Vero Beach.

"Doesn't look like you're having much success," says the woman who promised to love, honor and field my two-hoppers.

"Oh, I don't know. If she can hit a curveball, I think we've got something here."

"Why don't you do with her what you do with the kids when they won't take their medicine?" she suggests.

"I don't know. Do you really think it's going to worry her if I threaten to take her bike away for a week?"

"I didn't mean that. I meant hide the pill in a piece of food."

"It's worth a try, I suppose. I'll hide it in a piece of cheese. Dogs love cheese."

I stick the pill into a small chunk of colby cheese that sells for $3.29 a pound. Eagerly, she takes the cheese. Her tail wags happily. It still is wagging happily when the pill drops out of her mouth. Eight dollar's worth of cheese later, she accidentally swallows the pill. That should take care of the infection.

Of course, by this time her cholesterol count probably is in the red zone. Fortunately, they have pills for that.

Unfortunately, they don't seem to have any pills for the fleas that she picks up by running around in the woods that summer.

The arrival of the fleas is greeted with semi-hysteria by the woman who promised to love, honor and tug on my leash. Not that I am surprised by that. She's not too wild about some of the friends I bring home, either.

So we pay to have the dog "dipped" in a special solution at the vet's, and we buy some bug bombs, and for the next three days both the house and the dog smell like the inside of a can of Raid.

And on the fourth day she informs me that the fleas are back.

"How do you know?" I ask.

"I just saw the six-year-old scratching behind his ear. With his hind leg."

"Maybe we should have him dipped."

"That's not going to help. They're all through the house."

"Maybe we should have the house dipped."

"Don't be ridiculous. We're going to have to call an exterminator."

I call an exterminator.

"Hello," I say to the lady who answers, "I have fleas."

"Have you been running around in the woods?" she asks.

"I mean my house has fleas."

"Oh, I see. Did you want someone to come out and kill them?"

"Not necessarily. Maybe you could just send out somebody to beat them up. Sometimes all you have to do is break a few of their kneecaps and . . ."

"There's no need to be sarcastic, sir."

"I'm sorry. But things are getting out of control here. Even as we talk my wife is measuring the kids for flea collars."

The woman lists the rates for having our house sprayed for fleas.

"That sounds awfully expensive," I say. "Don't you have anything cheaper?"

"Oh, certainly, sir. We have a special $10 rate."

"That sounds pretty good."

"Fine, sir. Just load the fleas into your car and drive them over here. We'll take care of the rest." She has a lot of nerve calling *me* sarcastic.

I agree to pay the extra amount for a house call.

"Uh, there's just one more thing," I say. "You see, we just bought this house, and it's in a nice neighborhood, and we're not real eager to let the neighbors know we have bugs and, well, I guess I'm just trying to make sure you'll be, you know, discreet."

"You have nothing to worry about," she assures me.

Two days later the van from the exterminating company pulls up and parks in our driveway. It is painted a very discreet shade of red. With a picture of a dead bug painted on the side in bright yellow. Right next to the four-foot-high sign saying: BUG EXTERMINATOR. The only thing missing is a neon sign and a marching band.

"I don't think this is going to help our status in the neighborhood," I say to the woman who promised to love, honor and meet me on the Main Line. "Not that we've ever been totally accepted, anyway."

"I tried to tell you," she replies, "this isn't the kind of neighborhood where you could plant tomatoes in the front yard."

The exterminator rings the doorbell. I answer it.

"You the folks with the bugs?" he asks.

"Yes, come in," I say, holding out my hand. "I'm Jed Clampett, and this is my wife, Granny."

The exterminator gives me a funny look.

"Is everything set?" he asks.

"Right," I say.

All morning we have been preparing the house. All the furniture has been moved at least six inches away from the walls. All the food has been covered. Everything has been picked up off of the floor, even stuff under the bed. Crawling under our bed to dig out all those things was a real chore. On the other hand, it was nice to finally find out where that turtle got to.

The exterminator tells us to leave the house for three hours. When we come back, he hands us a bill for $70 and says that should take care of the problem.

Ten days later I haven't actually seen any fleas in our house, though I am itching a lot. But I am careful not to let her see me scratching. Because I know who would be the next to get dipped.

Even when she isn't bugging our house, the dog can be a real problem. If I had to do it over again, I would never buy a white dog.

Dirt shows on white dogs. Sure, lint shows on black dogs, but that's easy to take care of. You can just sneak up on a black dog while it's sleeping, turn on the vacuum cleaner and give it a good shot with the drapery attachment.

But white dogs have to be cleaned, because they show every spot of grease, used bubble gum and chocolate ice cream that comes within 100 yards of them.

Which doesn't bother me all that much but seems to irritate the woman who promised to love, honor and fill my water bowl.

"That dog is a mess," she complains one day. "She has spots all over her. When are you going to do something about it?"

"I am doing something about it. I'm telling everybody that she's a Dalmation."

"That's not what I had in mind. I meant, when are you going to give her a bath? Not only does she look grungy, she's starting to smell pretty gamey. Or hadn't you noticed?"

"Of course I noticed. I just didn't realize that she was the cause of the smell."

"Where on earth did you think it was coming from, then?"

"I had it narrowed down to the nine-year-old's closet or the bottom of the refrigerator."

"Well, it's coming from that dog, and you'd better do something about it or the two of you are going to be bunking together tonight."

I call for the dog, who is sleeping peacefully in the living room. Reluctantly, she gets up and slinks and dribbles her way into the kitchen, her tail clamped between her legs. She may not be real smart, but she has enough brains to realize that she is not being awakened because we have an extra pound of sirloin that we don't know what to do with. The last time we woke her up, in fact, was so we could take her to be wormed and neutered. With memories like those, I'd slink and dribble, too.

Now that I have her attention, I have to figure out what to do with her. It's too cold to bathe her outside, and the dishwasher is already full. My best bet seems to be the tub in the laundry room.

I coax her into the laundry room and run lukewarm water into the tub until it is about one-third full. Now all I have to do is get her into the tub. The trouble is that she is at that in-between size: too small to jump into the tub herself but big enough to cause hernias in a lifter.

Thankful that she still has her tail clamped between her legs, I stick a hand under each end and hoist her into the tub. Her growls are just loud enough to drown out the popping sounds in my back.

Once she is in the tub, I discover that the water level comes up only to her chest, leaving her upper half entirely dry.

"I don't suppose you'd consider lying down in the water on your back?" I ask her.

Trembling and dribbling, she looks up at me silently. I get the distinct impression that she is trying to give me a message. Fortunately, dogs do not have fingers.

I leave her there, trembling and dribbling, while I go in search of something with which to pour water over her back. When I return, the tub is about half full. With a plastic mug, I scoop a cupful of water onto her back. With a quick shake, she sprays a cupful of water into my face. I scoop. She shakes. I scoop again. She shakes again. In no time at all she is entirely wet. Which gives her a lot in common with me, the entire laundry room and half of the adjoining kitchen.

I wash and rinse her thoroughly. When I am finished, I lift her out of the tub and rub her with an old towel. It is impossible to get all of the water out of her fur, but it's warm in the house and she should be dry by the end of an hour. The laundry room carpet, on the other hand, may not be dry by the end of the year.

I clean up the laundry room and go into the living room, where the six-year-old is watching television.

"Where's the dog?" I ask him. "I thought she'd be in here rubbing up against the couch to get dry."

"She was," he says. "But she's in the basement now. I fixed her a snack for being a good girl and taking her bath."

"That was very nice of you. What did you give her?"

"A big bowl of chocolate ice cream."

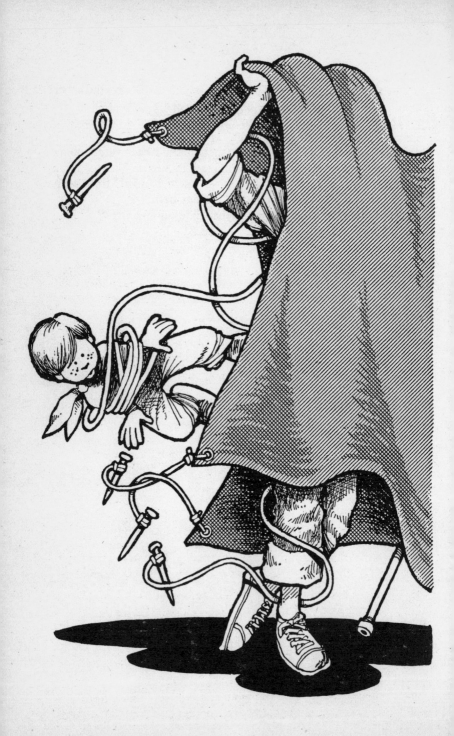

4

Cub Scouts (and other oaths)

And still our family continues its mysterious growth.

The woman who promised to love, honor and be fruitful blames it on my job.

"If you didn't take so many trips and work so late, I wouldn't need so many kids around to keep me company," she insists.

"If we didn't have so many kids, I wouldn't take so many trips and work so late," I point out.

Whatever the cause, I am now the father of three: An 11-year-old, an eight-year-old and a baby. The 11-year-old has the phone tied up in giggles whenever I try to call home. The infant makes funny little grunting sounds and develops a peculiar aroma whenever I hold him on my lap. But it's the eight-year-old who gives the most trouble. The eight-year-old is a Cub Scout.

Having grown up in a neighborhood where the only kids in uniforms we ever saw had just escaped from somewhere, I never knew much about Cub Scouting. And I didn't know anything at all about the Pinewood Derby.

The idea of the Pinewood Derby is for each Cub Scout and his dad to get together and build a little model car, which then is raced when all the Dens gather for the monthly Pack meeting. The racing is not the important part, of course. The important part is the time spent together by the Cub Scout and his dad, time which will help cement the vital relationship between father and son that leads to a full and rewarding life when the youngster matures into an honest, hard-working, clear-eyed adult.

Apparently it works. The Cub Scouts have statistics to prove that no boy who participated in the Pinewood Derby ever grew up to be a chain saw murderer.

And so the first year our Cub Scout brings home his Pinewood Derby kit, we rush down to the basement, where we spend an hour and a half together: Five minutes reading the instructions, 10 minutes sanding the wood, 10 minutes spray painting the wood, 10 minutes assembling the parts, 10 minutes re-reading the instructions, 15 minutes taking off the wheels and putting them back on the right way and 30 minutes arguing about which end is the front.

At the Pack meeting that year, while I watch hopefully, our car finishes fourth out of the six in our Den.

But on the way home, our Cub Scout says to me:

"That's all right, I don't care if we didn't win. I still think you're the best dad in the whole wide world."

The second year our Cub Scout brings home his Pinewood Derby kit, we hurry down to the basement, where we spend two hours together: 30 minutes sanding, 15 minutes spray painting, 15 minutes assembling and an hour discussing why it's all right for a grownup to say words like that when the electric sander slips and grinds all the hair off the back of his left hand.

At the Pack meeting that year, while I watch uncomfortably, our car finishes fifth out of the six in our Den.

But on the way home, our Cub Scout says to me:

"That's all right, I don't care if we didn't win. I still think you're a pretty good dad."

The third year our Cub Scout brings home his Pinewood Derby kit, we saunter down to the basement, where we spend two and a half hours together: 30 minutes sanding, 30 minutes spray painting, 30 minutes assembling and an hour explaining to the woman who promised to love, honor and spin my wheels how it was possible to get red spray paint on the inside of her washing machine.

At the Pack meeting that year, while I watch miserably, our car loses every race.

And on the way home, our Cub Scout says to me:

"Boy, Keith sure is lucky. His dad never helps him with his car."

So on the fourth year our Cub Scout brings home his Pinewood

Derby kit, we throw it down the basement stairs and forget all about it until the day before the race. That evening we spend three and a half hours together: 10 minutes sanding, 10 minutes spray painting, 10 minutes assembling and three hours watching the Pro Bowl on television.

The next day our Cub Scout turns up sick and it is decided that whatever he has probably is not needed at the Pack meeting. So we send the car along with another father to be raced.

At the Pack meeting that year, while I sit home watching *Happy Days,* our car wipes out all of its challengers and wins first place for the entire Derby, earning for us a large trophy.

It is the first trophy ever won by anyone in our family and I am sort of upset that neither of us is there to receive it. On the other hand, I'm relieved that we did win. For his birthday, our Cub Scout has been asking for a chain saw.

Despite my best efforts, our Cub Scout remains in the program and the next thing I know, I am a Den leader.

Becoming a Cub Scout Den leader is not something you plan. It just sort of happens to you. Like hemorrhoids. One day you are spending your Monday evenings with Frank and Howard and Dandy Don and the next thing you know you are standing with three fingers in the air promising to do your best to do your duty.

I'm not sure how it happened to me. I'm not sure I even want to think about it. All I know is that suddenly I am a co-leader for Webelos Den 4, Pack 234.

Webelos, incidentally, are 10-year-olds who are making the transition from Cub Scouts to Boy Scouts. They are at that in-between stage. Too old to sit around the campfire with their mothers, but too young to care about where the Girl Scouts' showers are.

The word "webelo" comes from the old Potawatomi word "webel," which means, "turn your back on 'em for a second and they'll break every stick of furniture in your teepee." The old Potawatomis knew which end of the papoose to paddle. That's how they managed to get old.

The first Den meeting is held in our basement. It is attended by 10 Webelos. Before the next meeting, three of them will drop out. Unfortunately, my kid is not one of them.

As suggested in the Webelo Leader's Book, we start the meeting with the Pledge of Allegiance to the Flag. More or less. The problem is, we don't actually have a flag, so we have to improvise. I'm not sure national headquarters would approve of our substitute. On the other hand, there's nothing in the Webelo Leader's Book that says we CAN'T pledge allegiance to a Cincinnati Bengals' pennant.

Carrying through on the patriotic theme, I start a discussion about the National Anthem.

"Does anybody know what the "Star Spangled Banner" is?" I ask.

"Sure," says a red-haired Webelo, "that's the song they play at baseball games."

In subsequent weeks, the meetings fall into a smooth routine: Open the meeting. Pledge allegiance to the Cincinnati Bengals. Take attendance. Collect dues. Discuss a topic in the Webelo's Scout Book. Play a game. Eat cookies and drink Kool-Aid. Adjourn the meeting. Let everyone out the front door. Let Jeff back in the front door to get his hat. Let Jeff out the front door. Let Jimmy back in the front door to get his Webelo's Scout Book. Let Jimmy out the front door. Let Scott back in the front door to get his brother. Let Scott and his brother out the front door. Lock the front door. Disconnect the doorbell. Send the dog down to the basement to clean up the cookie crumbs.

After three months of this, I decide that what Den 4 needs is to take a field trip in lieu of one of its regular meetings. Not that the meetings are all that tough. But the door knob is wearing out. And the dog is getting awfully fat.

I bring up the subject during a Den meeting. "If you guys had your choice for a field trip, where would you like to go?"

"Hawaii."

"The Super Bowl."

"An X-rated movie."

I point out to the guy who suggests Hawaii that it would cost too much money to go there. I point out to the guy who suggests the Super Bowl that the game was played three weeks ago. I point out to the guy who suggests the X-rated movie that I wasn't really asking for suggestions from the other Den leaders.

After considerable discussion, we narrow the field trip down to two choices: We can go on a tour of a local television station or we can visit the public library and see a slide presentation on the development and evolution of the Dewey decimal system.

We decide to visit a local television station. The vote is 5 to 4.

On the eve of the Den's field trip to the local television station, the other Den leader, who had agreed to go along and help keep things under control, calls to say that he will be unable to make it. An unexpected medical problem has cropped up, he explains. Not being a suspicious person, I have no reason to doubt him. On the other hand, I have never heard of an emergency vasectomy.

But it's too late to change plans. It will be me against half a dozen 10-year-olds. I console myself with a favorite homily:

"Though you be outnumbered, fear not, for the wisdom of your years shall prevail against the overwhelming numbers of your enemy."

A famous military man said that. Just before he led his troops into Little Bighorn.

The next day I pick up the six Webelos after school and we drive to the local television station. As we drive, I ask them which local television personality they most want to meet. They are divided. One votes for the weatherman. One votes for the sports director. Four vote for Kermit the Frog.

We arrive at the television station at 3:48, which is quitting time there. I know it is quitting time there, because just as we come in the front, I see a whole bunch of people hurrying out the back.

Inside, we are greeted by a man who says he will be our guide. He is not the regular guide, he adds, holding his short straw in a trembling hand. The regular guide called in a few minutes ago with an unexpected medical problem.

"Emergency vasectomy?" I ask.

"She didn't say."

We start our tour in the advertising department, where each Webelo is given an advertising handbill, suitable for hanging, framing or collecting autographs. Then we tour the weatherman's office, where each Webelo is given a weather map that actually was used on the air. The weather maps are suitable for hanging, framing or rolling up into swords.

We sword-fight our way through the business offices, past the control room and into the newsroom, where we meet a real television reporter who is busily engaged in preparing for the 6 o'clock program of award winning electronic journalism.

"Webelos, huh?" he says, putting down his hot comb. "What do you call this group? A Den? A Pack?

"A herd," our guide answers.

The tour lasts 45 minutes. But it seems a lot longer. Time tends to pass slowly when you expect at any moment to hear the sound of a shattering $1,500 video recorder and you're trying to keep six rolled-up weather maps from being crammed into the film developing machine.

Eventually the tour ends. We thank our guide and head for the car.

"That was neat," one of the Webelos says.

"Yeah," another agrees. "Let's take a field trip again next week."

"Sorry, boys," I say, "I won't be able to take you."

"Why not?"

"I feel an unexpected medical problem cropping up."

Of course, scouting is more than Pinewood Derbies, Den meetings and field trips to television stations. Scouting is packing up the old mess kit and hiking along forest trails with a song in your heart, a smile on your lips and a thorn in your foot. Scouting is a camp-out in the woods.

It is the woman who promised to love, honor and keep my firewood dry who reminds me of our Cub Scout's annual camp-out.

"Sounds great," I say. "Sleeping under the stars. Waking up at the crack of dawn. Fishing in clear streams in the fresh, pure air. Perhaps he'll see a raccoon. Some squirrels. A tiny little chipmunk."

"It's a father-son camp-out this year," she says.

"Of course you know there's bears in those woods. Big hairy man-eaters. And mountain lions. And gorillas. And sharks. And . . ."

"Are you trying to say you don't want to go?"

"Listen, if God intended man to sleep outside, why did He invent mosquitoes?"

"But if you don't go camping with your son, how do you expect to develop a rapport with him? Go on this camp-out together and I guarantee that you'll develop a common interest."

"Yeah, we'll both learn to hate camping. So just forget it. I'm not going camping and I don't want to hear another word about it."

Wordlessly, she walks to the family room. Wordlessly, she begins to make up the daybed for me. Wordlessly, I pack my knapsack.

That weekend we drive to Camp Birch. Several other fathers and sons already are there when we arrive. One father is busy making a fire. I am somewhat surprised by this, seeing as it is in the middle of the afternoon and the temperature is in the 80s.

"Why are you making a fire?" I ask him.

"I don't know," he says. "It's just that you always make a fire when you set up camp. It's like boiling water when somebody's going to have a baby."

Another father has brought the two tents that we will call home for the next few nights. They are four-man tents. Which is not to imply that four men can fit into them. A four-man tent is one that takes four men to put up. Fortunately, we have four men available. Unfortunately, they are the wrong four men. After half an hour of sweating, straining, fumbling and Cub Scout oaths, we decide to read the directions.

Eventually the tents are up. It is time to begin the father-son activities. And so we fish. We hike. We practice ax-handling skills. Before I know it, an hour has passed.

By nightfall, all the activities in the fresh forest air have worked their magic. Little heads begin to nod around the campfire. Tired little legs carry weary little bodies to their sleeping bags before 10 o'clock. The kids, on the other hand, stay up all night.

The next morning we are up at the crack of dawn. Sunrise, I discover, looks just like sunset. Only it's on the other side. We have breakfast: Pancakes, bacon and shooting pains, prepared over a crackling propane stove.

Not long after breakfast comes the part I have been dreading. Taking one last breath of fresh forest air, I enter the building at the edge of the campsite. It is what they call a primitive facility, just like the pioneers used. After being in there for a few minutes, I begin to understand why the pioneers were always moving on.

The rest of the day is spent in more fishing, hiking and ax-handling. In the afternoon, a Boy Scout comes along and shows us how to prepare our dinners so that they can be cooked directly on the hot coals of the campfire.

"Just wrap the foil real tight, put the food on the coals and in 15 or 20 minutes you'll have the best dinner you ever tasted," he assures us.

At 6 o'clock we place our tightly-wrapped foil dinners on the hot coals of the campfire. At 6:05 it begins to rain.

As we sit in our tent, muddy, itchy and hungry, watching the best dinners we were ever going to taste sinking into a pool of soggy ashes, the 10-year-old turns to me.

"Just think, dad, this is my last year in Cub Scouts. We'll never get to do this again."

"Stiff upper lip, son."

"Yeah. Next year I'll be in Boy Scouts. When we get to come here for a whole week."

If nothing else, three years in Cub Scouts proves to be a learning experience. He learns how to get wet every piece of clothing he has brought along five minutes after we arrive at a remote campsite, how to start a fire so that the smoke always blows into the tent, and how to tie a rope around his sleeping bag with a knot that won't come undone until we are in the station wagon on the way home.

I learn never to volunteer.

At first, I seemed to always be volunteering. When a driver was needed to take the Den to the Natural History Museum for a slide show on the history of Indian moccasins, it always was my car they went in. When just one more adult had to be found to take the Pack on an overnight hike across the Mojave Desert, I was the one who was found. The strange thing is, I don't ever remember raising my hand.

But with experience comes wisdom. Not to mention excuses. By the third year I have become a veteran of avoidance. A master of the side-step. Whenever the word "volunteer" is mentioned, I am able to instinctively look at my calendar, shake my head and announce that on that date I would be: (A) out of town, (B) in the hospital for major surgery or (C) at the funeral of a loved one.

But there are some close calls.

On a cold Friday night that winter, for instance, the woman who promised to love, honor and warm my pup tent mentions that tomorrow is the day of the Cub Scouts' annual Winter Olympics.

"So, why are you telling me?"

"Our Den needs drivers to take them there."

"Sorry. I'm going to the funeral of a loved one at an out-of-town hospital."

"Don't give me that. All you're planning on doing Saturday afternoon is sitting around and watching stupid football games."

"I know that. But the other parents in the Den don't. Let some of them drive."

"I've already called around. One father agreed to take half the kids. But every other father in the Den is scheduled for major surgery on Saturday."

"Boy, can you believe the deceit of some people? But I don't care. I'm still not driving."

"You've got to. If you don't, the 10-year-old will miss the Winter Olympics."

"So?"

"So, he won't get his Snowman Badge."

"So?"

"So, it probably will scar him for the rest of his life. Children who are denied the opportunity to achieve success within their peer groups frequently develop neuroses that disturb their later development and cause them conflicts in their adult lives, which often manifest themselves in violent, antisocial behavior. John Wilkes Booth never got the chance to earn his Snowman Badge."

It's hard to argue with a woman who majored in creative history. I agree to drive the 10-year-old and half the Den to the Winter Olympics. If only to save the life of a future president.

Saturday morning dawns bright and clear. Clear enough to see that the thermometer outside the kitchen window registers 12 degrees.

"It could be worse," points out the woman who promised to love, honor and boil my mercury. "It could be snowing."

Ten minutes later it begins snowing.

"Maybe they'll cancel because of the snow," I say.

"They hardly ever cancel a Winter Olympics because of too much snow," she points out.

There is nothing to do but get dressed. The 10-year-old puts on his quilted, down-filled, scientifically designed ski suit, the one that would keep him warm if he had to spend the winter on Neptune.

I, unfortunately, do not have a quilted, down-filled, scientifically designed ski suit. What I do have is three pairs of socks, a tennis warm-up suit, a purple turtleneck sweater, a green sweatshirt and a pair of worn Levis with a hole in the crotch.

I put them all on, waddle outside and we get into the car. We drive to the parking lot where we are supposed to meet the other members of our Den. There will be five kids in my car and five in the other father's car.

When we arrive, the other father already is there with two kids. I have never met him before. This must be his first year as a Scout father.

"Where are the rest of the kids?" I ask.

"They're late," he says. "The Pack leader said to wait until 11:30. If they're not here by then, we should leave without them."

We sit in our cars and wait. At 11:29 I point out to the other father that it looks like the other kids aren't coming.

"Guess not," he says. "Looks like we're just going to have these kids to take. It seems sort of silly to use two cars to take three kids, doesn't it?"

"My thought exactly," I agree, shoving my 10-year-old into the backseat of his car. "Gosh, I really appreciate your volunteering to take them. If I leave now, I think I can still get to the funeral on time."

At 11:30.01 I am out of the parking lot, driving back home. I feel sort of guilty about sticking him with the driving like that.

On the other hand, I have just passed along a lesson it took me three years to learn. I look at it as my good deed for the day.

But there are some lessons I never seem to absorb.

When I hear the word "banquet," I still picture elegantly dressed men and women being served beef Wellington by white-gloved waiters, pausing occasionally to exchange bons mots or cleanse their palates with Chateau Latour. All of which takes place in elegant surroundings, with gentle music in the background. Subdued lighting. Fine china. Expensive silverware. Nancy Reagan on my left. Ronald Reagan on my right. Ronald Reagan on everybody's right.

It is a fantasy that has survived approximately half a million Blue and Gold Banquets.

The Blue and Gold Banquet is a covered-dish event held each year to recognize the fact that the Pack has reached that point in the year that is exactly halfway between the Pinewood Derby and the Sailboat Regatta. Then again, it could be merely a show of support for the Fried Chicken Workers of America.

At any given Blue and Gold Banquet, 75 of the 100 covered dishes carried in will contain fried chicken. The rest will contain lime Jell-O. It's getting so that every time I see a fried chicken leg I automatically stand, hold up three fingers, recite the Pledge of Allegiance and sing two verses of "My Country 'Tis of Thee."

"I don't understand why everybody has to bring chicken," I say to the woman who promised to love, honor and cook my gizzard as we are preparing for the banquet. "One of these times I'm going to show up with a covered dish full of corned beef and see what happens."

"You always were a troublemaker," she says. "Now let's get going before we're late. And don't forget the Jell-O."

We drive to the Colonel's, buy a bucket, transfer the chicken to our covered dish and proceed to the banquet, which is held in the elementary school gym. It is not the elegant surroundings of my fantasy banquets. Even when it is decorated with blue and gold crepe paper, the elementary school gym still looks like the elementary school gym. Worse, it still smells like the elementary school gym.

An organizer meets us at the door.

"Chicken or Jell-O?" she asks, pointing to the covered dish I am carrying.

"Coquilles St. Jacques," I reply.

"Desserts go at the end of the table," she says.

I put the covered dish on a table between a platter of extra-crispy thighs and a casserole of golden brown breasts and take a seat at the table assigned to our Scout's Den. The banquet is scheduled to start at 6:30 sharp. It is 6:45. We are 15 minutes early.

A few witty bons mots might help pass the time. I turn to the person seated next to me.

"Did you hear what Art Buchwald said to Henry Kissinger at Sans Souci the other day?" I ask.

The person seated next to me is the little sister of a Scout in our Den. She appears not to have heard me. Possibly because she is digging something out of her ear with her thumb. Although I could be wrong about that. She could be putting something in. Either way, her interest in Art Buchwald's repartee appears to be minimal.

When it is time for the banquet to begin, the Scoutmaster announces that we will go through the food line one Den at a time. Our Den will be last.

We sit at our table, watching Scouts punch each other in the shoulder, while the other Dens go through the line. Finally, it is our turn. I carry my paper plate to the food table, where I discover that the bowls of Jell-O are warm and the bowls of fried chicken are empty.

I pour myself a serving of Jell-O and poke through the remains of the chicken. There are no more extra-crispy thighs. No more golden brown breasts. I have my choice of two extra-soggy wings or a piece of bird that I do not recognize. I think it is a foot.

I put the two chicken wings into the pool of Jell-O and carry them back to the table. By the time I get there, the Jell-O has started to eat through the bottom of the plate.

I stab at a wing with my plastic fork. Two of the three plastic tines snap off. With the remaining tine, I hold the chicken down while I saw at it with a plastic knife. The plastic knife cuts through the chicken, the liquid Jell-O and the paper plate.

Trying to ignore the green stain spreading out from underneath my plate, I eat the two chicken wings, pausing occasionally to cleanse my palate with warm Hawaiian Punch.

Ron and Nancy have no idea what they're missing.

After three years of Blue and Gold Banquets, field trips, father-son camp-outs and 3 a.m. trips to the edge of the woods, our oldest son tires of scouting. My sigh of relief is interrupted when our second son becomes a Cub Scout. With a vengeance.

Unlike our first son, who really only joined because he knew that they served cookies at the end of the meetings, our second son is filled with ambition, enthusiasm and energy. The neighbors figure he's adopted.

"He's really doing a great job," his mother points out. "All he needs now is some help from you on his merit badges. He has to learn knot-tying and working with tools."

"I don't know anything about that kind of stuff. Why don't you help him?"

"Because that's a father's job," she says.

"Where does it say that in the Equal Rights Amendment?"

"All right. If you're not interested in your son's development, just forget it," she says. "It's probably not important anyway."

"That's what I say."

"After all, there are lots of boys who grew up without being in Scouts. My cousin Billy was never a Scout, but he grew up just fine. In fact, he and his father have a terrific relationship today. Uncle John goes up to see him every month on visitor's day and they have a real nice talk. They say Cousin Billy has a terrific chance for parole after just . . ."

"Oh for heaven's sake. Tell him I'll work with him on tying knots after dinner."

That evening we go down to the basement to practice tying knots. After two hours we have used 27 feet of clothesline. On one knot.

"Are you sure that's the way it's supposed to look?" he asks, looking skeptically from the picture in the Scout manual to the tangle of clothesline on the basement floor.

"Well, if you're not sure, go ahead and untie it, and we'll start again," I tell him.

"Untie it? I can't even lift it."

The next evening we work on the use of tools in the garage, starting with the simple skill of driving a nail through a board. After 17 bent nails, eight split boards and a pair of purple thumbs, he taps me on the shoulder.

"What is it? I ask.

"Oh, nothing," he says. "I was just wondering when it was going to be my turn to try using the hammer."

Fortunately, most of his projects are done at Den meetings, and I never see them until they are finished. But even those create problems. Like the bird feeder, which he makes out of a bleach bottle and three sticks.

When it's all done he brings it home proudly, shows it to me and insists that that we have to hang it on a tree in the backyard right away so the neighborhood birds will have someplace to go for breakfast in the morning.

We go out into the backyard, he finds a tree he wants and I hoist him up on my shoulders to hang it on a branch. When he is finished, he jumps down from my shoulders. Just before the bird feeder lands on my head.

"How did you tie that thing?" I ask him.

"I used that knot you taught me the other night."

We tie the bird feeder again, using a triple knot to make sure it stays up there.

So now I have a bird feeder in my backyard. And birdseed in my hair. And birds that fly directly over my car's windshield after breakfast. And purple thumbs. And a clothesline that never will be untangled.

And, worst of all, a five-year-old who can't wait to grow up and become a Cub Scout, just like his brothers.

5

Vine–covered mortgage payments

In the 12th year of our connubial ecstasy, yet another child is born unto us. Our family tree is beginning to look like a forest.

"Do you know what we need?" asks the woman who promised to love, honor and sharpen my ax.

"Separate bedrooms?"

"Nope. A new place to live. This place just doesn't have enough space for all of us. We need a bigger house."

"Maybe we should have smaller children."

"I think we should build our own house," she continues, paying scant attention to what I consider an eminently sensible idea. "Something with lots of bedrooms and a family room with a fireplace in it and a formal dining room and a big lot in the suburbs."

"How do you expect us to be able to build something like that? In case you haven't noticed, I am not the world's handiest man. Remember that disaster I created with the power tools you gave me for Christmas?"

"Of course I do. And I thought it was a lovely footstool."

"It was a lamp."

"Well, anyway, that doesn't matter. You don't actually build the house yourself. You just pick out the floor plan and the colors and all that stuff and the builder puts it up for you. There's nothing to it."

She is right. Faster than you can say "lifetime of debt," we have moved into a new house with four bedrooms, a family room with a fireplace, a formal dining room and a big lot in the suburbs. The house is just as we had imagined it.

Except, maybe, for the patio.

When we discussed it with the builder, he said that the patio would be 30 by 40. It is not until after we move in that we discover he meant inches.

Sitting on a patio that is 30 by 40 inches is not impossible. It just takes a little adjustment. Which is what I point out to her as we are sitting back there one evening in our aluminum folding chair.

"That's easy for you to say," she says. "You're sitting on top."

So I decide to enlarge the patio. I have limited experience in the patio enlarging field, but how hard can it be? You simply level off an area, pour in some concrete and before you know it you're sitting on a patio listening to the soft summer breeze whispering through the weeping willow.

I start by digging up the area around the existing patio until I have a level space 10 feet wide, 20 feet long and five inches deep. Next, I put 2-by-4s around the perimeter, bracing them firmly. Bracing them firmly is very important. Otherwise, when the concrete is poured, you will wind up with a patio that is 90 feet wide, 110 feet long and one-eighth of an inch deep.

With my 2-by-4s firmly braced, I place a call to the nearest sand, gravel and concrete company.

"I want to buy some concrete," I say.

"How much do you need?"

"I'm not sure. What's the smallest amount I can get?"

"The minimum is three cubic yards, delivered for $90."

"Gosh, I was hoping I could get away for less than that. Don't you have anything cheaper?"

"Sure. How about our Floor-It Special? Three cubic yards for $24.95, plus FET and trade-in."

"That sounds better. But why do you call it the Floor-It Special?"

"Because at that price we don't deliver. We pour it into the trunk of your car and you try to make it home before it hardens."

"I guess I'll have it delivered."

A few days later a truck roughly the size of Yankee Stadium pulls up in front of the house. On the back, a gigantic mixer is churning away.

"I've got your concrete," says the driver. I'm glad he tells me that, because otherwise I might have mistaken him for the delivery boy from Luigi's Pizza.

"Where do you want me to dump it?" he asks.

"In the backyard."

"You mean the one with the split rail fence all around it?"

"Oh . . .yeah."

While he climbs back into his truck, I dismantle two sections of the fence. It is not a difficult process. I simply reverse the procedure I used three weeks ago when I put them up.

The truck drives across my lawn, leaving in its wake a perfect set of tire tracks. Ten inches deep. When it reaches the backyard, the driver jockeys the truck into position. Then he climbs out, maneuvers the chute at the back of the truck, climbs back into the cab and shifts some levers. The concrete begins to ooze out.

"How's it going?" he yells back to me.

"Not bad," I shout. "But I was sort of hoping you were going to pour the concrete inside the 2-by-4s."

Eventually we get the three cubic yards of concrete inside the 2-by-4s and the truck pulls out, flattening two bushes, one Big Wheel and a neighbor's garage. The neighbor is plenty mad about that. But that's what he gets for not leaving his car out in the driveway like everybody else on the block.

After a week of curing, settling and hardening, the patio is ready to use. It has been a tough job, but well worth it. There's a lot of satisfaction in sitting on the patio you made with your own hands, listening to the soft summer breeze whispering through the weeping willow tree . . . through the hole in your fence . . . through the ruts in your lawn . . . through the space where the neighbor's garage used to . . .

Inevitably the soft summer breezes turn into the cold advance men of approaching winter. Which is when we notice that in addition to not going overboard on the patio, our builder did not waste a great deal of the nation's precious supply of insulation in our house.

This fact is pointed out to me by the woman who promised to love, honor and keep the electric blanket turned to "braise."

"While you were at work today," she says, "the baby was walking past the door that connects the kitchen with the garage and a strong wind came along and actually knocked him down."

"You should keep that door shut," I say.

"It was."

"Oh."

"So, what are you going to do about it?"

"Buy him heavier shoes?"

"Very cute. But that's not going to help. I think you should put up a storm door between the kitchen and the garage."

"That's impossible. There's no way to attach a storm door there. Don't you remember? That was one of our options: We could either have the builder put a storm door between the kitchen and the garage or a roof over the living room."

"No problem," she says. "You can buy doors already prehung, with the frame and everything all together. I was talking with a salesman and he said that they're so simple to put up that a 10-year-old could do it."

"Great. If we wait two years, the eight-year-old can take care of it."

"That's it, Don Rickles, keep on with the jokes. Don't let it worry you that the wind is whipping through here like Hurricane Hattie and that we're the only ones on the block with frost on the outside of our refrigerator and that when the children get up in the morning I have to chip their little pajamas off of them with an ice pick and that . . . "

"All right, all right, I'll put up the stupid storm door. But you have to go and buy it."

"It's in the basement."

"What?"

"I bought it yesterday."

The storm door in the basement comes in a large, storm-door-sized carton. The directions are printed on the outside:

STEP 1—To open carton, carefully take tab "A" in your left hand and pull it slowly toward tab "B" with a gentle motion so as not to tear insert "1". When tab "A" and tab "B" have intersected at point "2", carefully extract the lower half of binder "C" with right hand while at the same time easing tab "D" into eyelet "E". When tab "D" is fully inserted into eyelet "E", break the hermetic seal on connector "3", using a 4 ¾₁₆ self-honing ground blade with offset grip only. (If not available, a potato peeler may be substituted.) When connector "3" is broken, remove door from carton, taking care not to damage nurled Z-bar "F".

STEP 2—Hang door.

To make Step 2 even simpler, the carton also contains a package of 17 Phillips screws to be inserted into the predrilled holes in the door. The 18 pre-drilled holes.

From my days at MIT, I recall that to insert a Phillips screw, you need a Phillips screwdriver. A hammer will not work. I look quickly through my toolbox. It's easy to look quickly through a toolbox that contains a hammer, three nails and a roll of Scotch Tape. The Phillips screwdriver is not there.

"Where's the Phillips screwdriver?" I yell.

"Philip who?"

"Not Philip. Phillips. The Phillips screwdriver."

"Is that the one with the little X on the end?"

"That's the one."

"It's in the cupboard, right next to the rolling pin. The 11-year-old needed it to decorate her Christmas cookies with little Xs."

"Oh . . . of course."

I blow the crumbs off of the Phillips screwdriver and begin to hang the door, inserting the 17 screws through the 18 pre-drilled holes. Six hours, 17 screws, three nails and a roll of Scotch tape later, the door is hanging. Not only is it hanging, it is hanging perfectly straight and it is easy to open.

Unfortunately, the doorway is crooked. The storm door will not close. From my days at BTU, I recall that a storm door that will not close isn't terribly effective at keeping out the cold.

But I'm not about to spend another six hours trying to fix it. Because, while I have been trying to hang the storm door, the woman who promised to love, honor and keep my foundation dry has discovered that the faucet in the backyard leaks.

"Who cares?" I say. "It's not going to hurt anything if it leaks back there. The water will run right down into the rose bush."

"Sure," she says, "until the cold weather hits. And then the water will freeze."

"Great. That will keep it from dripping."

"Sure. And the ice will back up into the pipes inside the house and eventually the pressure will be too much and the pipes in the house will rupture, which will probably happen while we're visiting my mother in Cleveland for Christmas and the water will pour out all over the house and we'll get back from Cleveland just in time to see your new stereo floating out of the living room window and . . ."

"I'll fix the damn faucet."

The next day I turn off the water in the basement, take my toolbox to the backyard and locate the faucet. It is leaking at the rate of about 20 drips a minute.

Although I have never attempted to repair an outdoor faucet, I am a veteran of countless battles with their illegitimate indoor cousins. The first step is to remove the handle. I reach into the toolbox for the tool which I have found to be the best suited for this purpose.

Five or six good raps with the hammer and the faucet handle is lying on the ground. It is in two pieces, I return the hammer to the toolbox. It is in three pieces.

With a borrowed wrench, I unscrew the nut that holds the faucet assembly inside the pipe. Unlike indoor faucets, in which the faucet assembly is just a few inches long, this one stretches 12 inches. At the very end is the little black rubber washer that is shirking its duty.

I drive to the hardware store, buy a new washer for 10 cents and return home. There I remove the old washer, put on a new one, reinsert the faucet assembly into the pipe, tighten the nut, walk downstairs to the basement, turn on the water, walk back upstairs to the backyard and check the faucet I have just repaired.

It is leaking at the rate of about 40 drips a minute.

Downstairs. Turn off the water. Upstairs. Remove the faucet assembly. Drive to the hardware store.

"If the washer didn't stop it, you probably need a whole new faucet assembly," the man there tells me. "I can let you have one for 10 bucks."

He lets me have one for 10 bucks. I drive home. Open the assembly. Try to fit it into the pipe. Discover that it won't fit. Kick the side of the house. Shove the old assembly back into the pipe. Limp downstairs. Turn on the water. Limp upstairs and go outside.

It is leaking at the rate of about 20 gallons a minute.

I return to the hardware store.

"This faucet assembly you sold me doesn't fit," I tell the man.

"I was afraid of that," he says. "What you're going to have to do is go inside the house to where that pipe comes in, take your torch and cut off the pipe, cut some new threads, get an adapter, slip the pipe into the . . ."

"Cut it with my what?"

"Your torch. You do have a torch, don't you?"

"No. Only a three-piece hammer."

"Well, don't worry. I can let you have one for $29.95."

"Forget it. I'll call a plumber."

"Suit yourself. Of course, he's gonna charge you 40 bucks just to pull into the driveway."

Obviously, I have a number of options.

I can call a plumber, who is going to stick me 40 bucks just for openers.

I can buy a $29.95 torch with which I can cut the pipe and very likely burn down the entire neighborhood.

I can let the faucet leak until it freezes. Which in turn will undoubtedly rupture every pipe in the house, ruining the entire contents.

I can sell my nearly new house and buy another one with faucets that do not leak, which, considering the various finance charges, would probably set me back no more than $40,000.

I can turn off the water for the winter and take lots of showers at the YMCA.

That's one of the nice things about building your own house. It gives you so much flexibility.

6

Hook, line and catfish

All my life I looked forward to the day that I would have a son old enough to take fishing.

I'm not sure why, exactly. It could be because most of my ideas of what being a father is all about come from Norman Rockwell paintings. Or maybe it's because my old man used to take me fishing when I was a kid. It was one of the few things we did together. Until I got old enough to drink.

Two or three times each summer we would get up while the sky was still black and the dew was heavy on the grass. We would get the lunches that we had packed the night before out of the refrigerator and we would climb into our '49 Plymouth and drive for miles to a new fishing hole my old man had heard about.

If I ever have a son, I promised myself after each of those trips, I'll take him fishing, too. And a feeling of warm anticipation would spread through me. There is a word for this feeling of warm anticipation. The word is "revenge."

I hated getting out of my comfortable bed in the middle of the night and getting the crummy sandwiches out of the refrigerator and driving for miles to some stupid place where the only thing biting was the mosquitoes.

So when our first son turns eight, I decide that it is time. He is at the perfect age for going fishing with his old man. Too old to need me to zip him up, but not old enough to tell me where I can cast my fishing rod.

I go out and buy two fishing outfits, complete with rods and reels and hooks and sinkers and half a dozen artificial lures that wouldn't fool any fish with half a brain. Not unless he was wearing dark glasses and carrying a white cane. And the next morning we get up while the sky is still black and the dew is heavy on the chickweed and we drive for miles to a lake that I have heard about.

By the time we arrive at the lake, the eight-year-old is really excited. I can tell that he is really excited by the way he keeps hopping up and down.

"Don't be impatient, son," I say with a paternal chuckle. "We'll have our lines in the water soon enough."

"I'm not impatient, Dad," he says.

"Sure you are, son. It's obvious to me that you are so excited about fishing that you can hardly stand still. Dads have a way of being able to tell these things."

"I'm not excited, Dad. Honest."

"Okay, son, have it your way. But, if you're not excited, then tell me why you're jumping up and down like that."

He tells me why he's jumping up and down like that. I tell him to try behind the big oak tree.

After he comes back out from behind the bit oak tree, we are ready to fish. Step-by-step, I instruct him in the ageless art of angling, drawing upon my years of experience. I show him the proper way to attach the hook. I show him the proper way to bait the hook. I show him the proper way to get the hook out of my thumb.

Then it is time to cast.

The sound of a gentle plop as my hook hits the water tells me that I have lost none of my casting ability. The sound of a second gentle plop a second later tells me that I have lost my worm.

Two dozen plops, seven snags and four trips to the big oak tree later, all we have caught is four pounds of seaweed and an inner tube. Just as we are about to leave, I feel a tug on my line. It could be a submerged tree branch, but I don't think so. If there is one thing I recognize, it is the feel of a submerged tree branch on my line.

Furiously, I begin to reel it in. The rod is bending. The line is straining. Suddenly, the fish is visible a few inches below the surface of the water.

"What is it, Dad?" the eight-year-old shouts.

"How the heck would I know? I never saw one up close like this before."

Then the fish is out of the water and flopping around on the ground. It is, without a doubt, the ugliest fish I have ever seen, a catfish with a huge, gaping mouth and a long, Fu Manchu mustache. There is something about that face that reminds me of a girl I used to date. Probably the mustache.

In any event, this is something upon which I had not counted. When my old man caught fish, he would simply slip them into the minnow bucket and nobody could tell the difference. As far as I could see, fishing was just another method of population control for night crawlers. It never occurred to me that I would actually catch something big enough to keep.

So we dig an old pail out of the trunk of the car, put some water in it, toss in the ugly fish and drive home. As I take the bucket out of the car and carry it into the kitchen, the fish still is splashing around in the water. After a moment of indecision, I empty the bucket into the kitchen sink. The water goes down the drain. The catfish continues flopping in the sink.

Just then I hear a familiar voice behind me. It is the woman who promised to love, honor and tug on my bobber.

"What do you think you're doing?" she yells.

"Great news. I caught this fish and I figure it's big enough for us to have it for dinner."

"It's still alive," she points out.

"I know. But it'll die in a few minutes. Then I'll cut it up and you cook it."

"You can't just let him sit there in the sink and suffer," she says.

"Maybe you're right," I agree. I take the fish out of the sink and put it on the carving board. With the sharpest knife I can find, I get ready to put the fish out of its misery. As I raise the knife, she cries out:

"Wait."

It is just like John Smith and Pocahontas, except that she doesn't lay her head on top of the fish's. Then again, Pocahontas wasn't married to the executioner, or she might have had second thoughts about that, too.

"Now what?" I demand.

"I don't want you to kill it."

"You want to kill it."

"No."

"You want me to put it back in the sink."

"No."

You want us to adopt it and let it stay in the spare bedroom."

"Of course not. I want you to put it in the tub in the basement."

"What's the difference if it flops around up here or down there?"

"I mean, put it in the tub with some water so that it can swim around. When it does die, then you can cut it up."

"What's it going to die of, lung cancer?"

But she convinces me to take the fish downstairs and toss it into a tub full of water. He is not flopping around as much as he was before. I don't think he understands it either.

Half an hour expires. An hour expires. The fish doesn't. As he continues flopping around in the tub, Pocahontas comes down to take a look. She smiles at the fish. When she starts talking to him, I know I've got problems.

She goes upstairs. A few minutes later she returns. In her hands she is holding firmly, but at arm's length, two large night crawlers.

"What are you doing?" I ask, not really sure I want to hear it.

"He looks hungry. I went out into the garden and dug him up something to eat."

"How could he be hungry? He just ate my bait two hours ago. Anyway, I'm hungry, too. What about me?"

"There's some leftover vegetable soup in the refrigerator."

I go upstairs and warm the soup. A few minutes later she comes back upstairs. In her hands, she is holding firmly, but at arm's length, two large, wet night crawlers.

"I guess he wasn't hungry after all," she says.

"Probably on a diet. So what are you going to do with the worms?"

"I'm putting them back in the garden. I think they were drowning."

She takes the worms outside. She is gone for quite a while. There can only be one logical explanation. She is giving them mouth-to-mouth.

Finally she returns.

"What took so long?"

"I wasn't sure they'd be able to get back underground. So I dug them a little hole to get them started."

"Good idea."

I finish my leftover soup. Then I go down to the basement. I scoop the fish out of the tub. I put him into a pail of water. I take the pail to the car. I drive the car to the lake. I take the pail out of the car. I throw the fish back into the lake.

Quickly the catfish swims away, apparently just as healthy as he was when I pulled him out. In fact, I wouldn't be surprised if he was still swimming around in that lake today. Unless, of course, he died laughing.

7
The
road show

For a long time after the catfish episode, I was convinced that the phrase "bad trip" meant taking your kid fishing.

Then I discovered family vacations.

At first, we could never afford to take family vacations. About all our budget could stand were short trips. In the afternoons, there were short trips to the swim club. In the evenings, there were short trips to the beer cooler. In the mornings, there were short trips to the medicine chest.

Just as I am growing accustomed to what I regard as a remarkably civilized arrangement, the whole thing is ruined by the woman who promised to love, honor and follow me to the ends of the Earth. Even if she has to drag me there.

"I suppose you heard that the Strombergs across the street went to Florida this year for their vacation?" she says, with the subtlety for which she is world famous.

"Oh, really?"

"Yes, really. And the Medlyns next door went to Michigan."

"Nice."

"And the Steadman's went to Virginia Beach."

When she gets to the part about how the Onassises went to Acapulco, I begin to notice a definite trend in the conversation.

"You're getting at something, aren't you?"

"What makes you say that?"

"Just a crazy hunch."

"Well, seeing as how you brought it up, I agree with you."

"About what?"

"That we should take a family vacation this year."

"Who said anything about taking a family vacation?"

"Why, you did, dear."

"Oh."

"Good, then that's settled. I'll start packing. This is going to be a real learning experience for all of us."

As she walks away to start packing, I'm still not convinced that taking the family on a vacation trip is a real great idea, but I'm willing to give it a try.

After all, it's so seldom that I can talk her into agreeing with me.

For our first family vacation, we pick Chicago. From where we live, it's not too far. And it's not too expensive. And there's nothing valuable there that our kids can break.

We decide to leave the one-year-old at home. The one-year-old tends to make even the shortest trips unpleasant. Not to mention aromatic. There is considerable discussion as to who should take care of the one-year-old while we are gone. We finally settle on Karen, who is our regular baby-sitter. But only because the Pittsburgh Steelers are busy.

As we pull out of the driveway, the woman who promised to love, honor and go out of her tree if she didn't get away from that kid for a few days begins to have second thoughts.

"Do you think he'll be okay?" she asks, anxiously. "What if he gets sick? Maybe we should take him along. Do you think Karen will be able to handle him?"

"Relax. Everything will be fine. Karen will be able to handle him."

"Are you sure?"

"Of course. Just as long as she doesn't untie him."

We drive to Chicago. The first thing we will visit, we have decided, is Chinatown.

"You know," I admit as we head for Chinatown, "you may have been right about this trip. I think the kids will get plenty of valuable learning experiences from this trip."

Her answer is drowned out by the funny noises being made in the backseat by the 12-year-old. The last time I heard funny noises like that was when the four-year-old decided to see if Italian salad dressing would do anything to liven up the taste of oatmeal.

By the time we arrive at the edge of Chinatown, the funny noises have subsided in the backseat and the 12-year-old insists that she is all right. We park the car. We clean out the backseat. We walk towards Chinatown.

Along the way we encounter a fire station. A friendly fireman is sitting in front of the fire station, just like in the coloring books.

"Who's that?" I say to the four-year-old.

"The friendly fireman," he says.

"That right. And do you know why he's sitting in front of the fire house?"

"Because he's on strike?"

The four-year-old has been reading too many newspapers.

The friendly fireman takes us on a tour of the fire house. The kids are full of questions.

"Where's the fire house doggie?" the four-year-old wants to know.

"Where's the fire house hoses?" the nine-year-old wants to know.

"Where's the fire house john?" the 12-year-old wants to know.

When the 12-year-old is finished making funny noises in the fire house john, we thank the friendly fireman and walk across the street to Chinatown.

Chicago's Chinatown is not nearly as extensive as the Chinatowns in San Francisco, New York or Peking. It consists mainly of one block of Chinese restaurants and gift shops. The Chinese gift shops sell Chinese souvenirs. Made in Japan.

We pause in front of one of the Chinese gift shops. Suddenly the 12-year-old makes a dash for the nearest doorway. As we rush to comfort her, we hear something behind us. It is the four-year-old. He is making funny noises, too. All over the sidewalk.

It is not the kind of picture you are likely to see on the cover of the Mobil Travel Guide. The 12-year-old is leaning over in a doorway. The four-year-old is leaning over at the curb. The nine-year-old is standing in the middle of the sidewalk, demanding to know how long it will be before dinner. A group of Chinese merchants are screaming "Sickies go home."

Despite this somewhat queasy introduction to family vacationing, the following year she wants us to try it again. So we decide to go to St. Louis. I'm not sure why we picked St. Louis. I mean, St. Louis has never done anything to us.

But on a hot summer morning, we pack the station wagon with four suitcases, one cooler, one potty chair, four sleeping bags, two cameras, 17 overdue library books, three dozen little plastic cars, eight coloring books and three boxes of crayons that will melt before we reach the city limits.

When all of this is stuffed into the station wagon, we are ready to take off for St. Louis. Or, rather, we would be ready to take off for St. Louis, except that now there is no room in the station wagon for the kids. A short but spirited discussion takes place. As usual, her suggestion overrules my suggestion.

"But I still think my idea was better," I say, as I rearrange things the way she wants them.

"Don't be ridiculous," she snaps. "Just how far do you think we'd get with four kids lashed to the top of the car?"

Finally we are off.

To reach St. Louis, you drive through Indiana and Illinois. Unless, of course, you live west of St. Louis, in which case driving through Indiana and Illinois is not necessarily the most direct route.

Indiana, the home of Earl Butz and the 500-mile left turn, is filled with impressive scenery. Especially if you are impressed by corn fields. After 150 miles of corn fields, we arrive at Turkey Run State Park, which is where we have reservations to spend our first night.

The Turkey Run State Park Inn, we discover, is just as the guide book described it: A rustic inn located in a tree shaded glen with a dining room that features open beam ceilings and lantern chandeliers. It is surrounded by 14 acres of scenic hiking trails. For once I have picked a perfect spot.

We check in and carry our bags to our room, which is on the second floor. Our room, we discover, comes complete with a rustic television set and a scenic view of the roof of the dining room that features open beam ceilings and lantern chandeliers.

Selecting a spot to eat that night is simplified by the fact that we are located deep in the heart of a state park. We can either eat in the inn's dining room or we can go out into the woods and wrestle a bear for his roots and grubs.

The food at the inn is simple fare but wholesome. The special of the evening is turkey, which comes with mashed potatoes, stuffing, green beans, salad and packaged breadsticks with ants in them.

Fortunately, I have eaten only half of my package of breadsticks when the 13-year-old notices the ants.

"Which way are they going?" I ask her, not wanting to look.

"What do you mean, which way?"

"I mean, are they going in or out?"

"Out."

"Oh boy."

We finish our meal. Except for the breadsticks. When we are done, I take our bill to the cashier.

"That will be $18.41," she says. "And how was your meal?"

"The breadsticks had ants in them."

"Your change is $1.59," she says. "Have a nice evening."

We leave the dining room with its antsy breadsticks and its wildly disinterested cashier. Outside, it is getting dark, but there still is enough light for a quick hike on some of the 14 miles of scenic trails. I head for the door. The rest of our hikers head for our room.

"Wait a minute, you guys," I call after them, "you're going the wrong way. The 14 miles of scenic hiking trails are this way."

"Are you kidding?" the 10-year-old calls back, "it's almost time for *Fantasy Island.*"

While the 14 miles of scenic trails sit outside, unhiked, we sit inside our room in the rustic inn and watch *Fantasy Island*, which is a show about how people can have their wildest, most far-fetched fantasies come true.

Someday, I vow, as I watch a man turned into a king and a woman who becomes a fashion model, I am going to submit a script for that show. It will be about this father, see, and his fantasy is to take his family on a vacation where the scenery is great and the food is terrific and after dinner they all go out into the woods for a hike and not one kid ever hits his brother with a melted crayon and . . . oh, forget it. They'd never go for anything that far out.

The next day we arrive in St. Louis.

St. Louis is a metropolitan area of 2,400,000 persons, 500,000 of whom live in another state. It is located in eastern Missouri on the west bank of the Mississippi, although East St. Louis is located in western Illinois, on the east bank of the Mississippi. This situation is so confusing to local residents that 200,000 of them don't live there anymore.

Although many people believe that St. Louis was named in honor of a fleet-footed outfielder who formerly played for the local baseball corporation, this is not true. In reality, St. Louis was named for King Louis IX of France, who led his country into three wars during the 13th Century and was, therefore, declared a saint.

The city of St. Louis was founded in 1764 by Pierre Laclede

Liguest, who had nothing better to do. Other great moments in St. Louis history include: 1822 (St. Louis becomes a city); 1904 (the World's Fair and Olympic Games are held in St. Louis); 1927 (the locally financed *Spirit of St. Louis* crosses the Atlantic); and 1953 (the St. Louis Browns move to Baltimore).

There are several worthwhile tourist attractions in St. Louis. One is Grant's Farm, a 281-acre area which offers free beer at the end of its tour. Another is the Anheuser-Busch brewery, a registered National Historic Landmark, which offers free beer at the end of its tours. St. Louis also has 3,000 manufacturing plants, none of which offer free beer at the end of their tours and are, therefore, hardly ever visited by tourists.

It is after our sixth tour of the Anheuser-Busch Brewery that the woman who promised to love, honor and hitch up my Clydesdales suggests that perhaps we should visit some other St. Louis landmarks. We decide to visit the Gateway Arch.

The Gateway Arch, known formally as the Jefferson National Expansion Memorial, is a monument to Thomas Jefferson, the pioneer spirit and cheap hamburgers. Rising 630 feet above the Mississippi, it is described as "the nation's tallest and most elegant memorial."

To reach the top of the Gateway Arch, you stand in line for half an hour to buy a ticket. This ticket entitles you to wait two hours for the tiny elevator that will take you to the top. At the top, there are 16 observation windows, through which you can see sights as far away as 30 miles. Which is roughly one-fifth as far as you could have driven if you hadn't waited two and a half hours to get up there.

After our two-and-a-half-hour wait, we squeeze into our seats on the elevator car and begin the four-minute ride to the top. Halfway up, I glance at the woman who promised to love, honor and get high with me. Her eyes are closed and there is a little smile on her face. It is obvious that she is enjoying the ride.

When we reach the top, the elevator stops and the door opens. Her eyes still are closed and there is still a little smile on her lips. There is a good reason for this. At the top of the nation's tallest and most elegant memorial, she has passed out.

With the help of two guards, I get her through the crowded observation deck to a private bathroom, where a vial of smelling salts revives her.

"Are you all right?" I ask.

"I'm fine," she says. "It must have been the thin air up here. Let's go back down."

We take the first car back down. As we descend, it occurs to me that, after a two-and-a-half-hour wait, we never did get to see the view from the world's tallest and most elegant memorial. On the other hand, we probably are the only family on our block to have seen the inside of the private bathroom at the top of the world's tallest and most elegant memorial.

After two consecutive summers spent proving that family vacations were invented by the devil on one of his grouchy days, I am in no mood to try another.

So on the first day of my vacation the following year, when she suggests that we drive somewhere I say:

"Oh no you don't. This year I'm staying home and drinking beer and watching games on television. And if you don't like it, you can just lump it, fatso."

On the second day of my vacation, the TV repairman comes. He says he can't recall ever seeing an entire six-pack embedded in a television chassis before.

On the third day of my vacation, we drive to Cleveland, which is 200 miles away as the crow flies. Unless the crow has four kids in the backseat and has to turn off at every third gas station.

On the fourth day of my vacation, we visit Grandma's. When we ring the doorbell, Grandma doesn't answer. So we open the door with our spare key and find her hiding in a closet, pretending that she doesn't want to see us. But we know that she is only fooling. We know that Grandma loves to have us come and visit her in her one-bedroom apartment and it doesn't bother her a bit if sometimes the pretty china figurines that she has had ever since she was a little girl get knocked off the shelf by a Frisbee.

On the fifth day of my vacation, we drive to Canada, the country that gives us hockey players and cold fronts. At the border a guard sticks her head in the front window and asks us some questions. Then she sticks her head in the back window. Then she pulls her head out again. Real fast. You'd think they'd teach them at border guard school not to stick their heads in cars that have four kids who ran out of Dramamine 100 miles ago.

On the sixth, seventh and eighth days of my vacation, we visit Toronto, which is a very nice city. Sort of like Detroit after a bath.

On the ninth day of my vacation, we visit African Lion Country

Safari in Rockton, Ont. It is one of those places where you can drive your car through for a close-up look at wild animals roaming free in simulations of their native environments. While we are there, a lion yawns, a rhino eats some grass and a monkey does a nasty thing on top of our car.

On the 10th day of my vacation, we drive back across the border, where a guard holds her breath and waves us through quickly.

On the 11th day of my vacation, we stop back in Cleveland, where Grandma is having the lock on her front door changed.

On the 12th day of my vacation, we arrive home.

On the 13th day of my vacation, I wash the nasty monkey stuff off the top of the car.

On the last day of my vacation, I smile a lot.

8

You gotta
have cheek

Shortly before she was about a year old, my first and only little girl held up her arms to me and smiled her sweetest smile and begged for a kiss. So I bent down to hug her plump little body and kiss her cute little face.

She bit me on the cheek.

From then on, we have what can only be described as a relationship of uneasy detente. She never really gave me a whole lot of trouble, I guess. Then again, I kept my cheeks protected at all times. Being the father of a boy is tough. Being the father of a girl is impossible.

Actually, for the first few years, there is hardly any difference between little girls and little boys. A healthy 10-month-old girl can knock a jar of strained apricots off of her high chair just as far as a 10-month-old boy. A two-year-old girl is the equal of any two-year-old boy when it comes to crayoning a rug, eating the contents of an ash tray or pulling up the neighbor's orchids. The differences come later.

When she is 13, for instance, my first-born informs me that she has qualified for free tickets under the Cincinnati Reds' "Straight A" program.

I have mixed emotions about this. I am pleased, naturally, that she is an honor student. On the other hand, I am underwhelmed at the thought of driving 120 miles round trip to watch a bunch of grown men stand around and spit. And I don't figure to get much help from the woman who promised to love, honor and never play out her option. Or, as she puts it when I ask her how she'd like to take the 13-year-old to a Cincinnati Reds game:

"You know I hate football."

So it is left to me to sit down with the 13-year-old and select which three games we will attend. The choices, I can't help but notice, are not all-inclusive. Conspicuous by their absence from the list of opponents are the Los Angeles Dodgers, Houston Astros, Pittsburgh Pirates or any other team that would recognize a World Series ticket. This is not unlike winning a free trip to anywhere in France except Paris. We wind up picking three games involving teams in imminent danger of being arrested for impersonating baseball players.

In the early summer we go to the first of our three free games.

The Cincinnati Reds transact their monopoly in Riverfront Stadium, a relatively new facility whose major distinction is that it looks almost exactly like every other relatively new facility around the country.

Seating is divided into four color-coded areas. At the bottom, nearest to where the men stand and spit, are the blue seats. Then comes the green seats. Then the yellow seats. Finally there are the "Ohmygod, George, I just saw an eagle with a nosebleed" seats. I first begin to suspect that our seats will be up there when I show an usher my ticket stubs and ask if he can guide us to them.

"No," he says, " but I can recommend a Sherpa guide who works cheap."

By the time we locate our aisle, climb the stairs, find our seats, shoo away the mountain goats and suck some oxygen, it is 20 minutes before game time. Just enough to fill in the 13-year-old on some of the basics of baseball.

I point out to her that the field is divided into two main areas: the infield and the outfield. In the infield there are four bases and an elevated area called the mound, upon which the pitcher stands for the purpose of humming them in there.

Taking the field first will be the home team, everyone of whom turned down a Rhodes Scholarship because he loves the game and lives only for the privilege of pleasing fans in this part of the country.

When their playing days are over, they all will settle down here and work for free with underprivileged children.

Batting first will be the visiting team, everyone of whom is a vicious, illiterate, not to mention illegitimate, degenerate who plays only for the thrill of intentionally maiming one of our players. When their playing days are over, they will return to their former jobs as ax murderers.

"Any questions?" I ask the 13-year-old after I have finished explaining the basics.

"Yes, I do have one."

"Ask away."

"Where are we stopping for dinner?"

"Is that the only thing you can think to ask after I have just spent 15 minutes explaining to you everything I know about baseball? If that's the best you can do, I can't imagine how you ever became an honor student."

"Well, I do have one question about your explanation. It's about that elevated area where the pitcher stands."

"Right. The mound. You want to know its exact dimensions. Well, it's 18 feet in diameter and it rises 10 inches high at the center."

"No, that's not what I wanted to know."

"What, then?"

"What I wanted to know is, instead of going to all that trouble to build a mound, why don't they just use taller pitchers?"

It's not an easy thing raising an honor student. I hope my parents realize how lucky they were never to have had that problem.

But baseball is only the beginning of the struggle.

That same year the woman who promised to love, honor and tickle my ivories decides that we need a piano in our house.

"Why?" I ask.

"For the 13-year-old," she says, producing statistics proving conclusively that the majority of girls who grow up with pianos in their homes never become unwed mothers, members of weird religious cults or contestants on the $1.98 Beauty Contest.

"I really don't think we can afford a piano," I say.

"I can get us one for free."

"Those are the most expensive kind."

But she goes ahead and gets the free piano anyway, which costs $45 to have delivered by two guys who bring it through the family room and leave it sitting in the kitchen.

"Wait a minute," I say, as they head back to their truck. "It doesn't go into the kitchen. It goes in the basement."

"Are you kidding, Mac?" one of them says. "Look at the size of that thing. You want that piano in the basement, the only way you're going to get it down there is to put it in the spot where you want it and then build a house over it."

What he says has the melody of truth. It is a rather large old upright. It is more than rather large. It is the Orson Welles of pianos. Families of 10 are living on farms in India that take up less space than that piano.

So we push it out of the kitchen and into the family room. Which is not a bad spot for it. Except that when the piano is sitting in the family room, the family can't.

After several weeks of watching television through binoculars, I decide that the piano is going into the basement. One way or another. With the aid of a hammer, two neighbors, three wrenches, four screw-drivers and five million dirty words, I disassemble that piano and carry it downstairs. Piece by piece. Key by key. The whole process takes a little longer than I had anticipated. But then, I really didn't have anything else planned for those three months anyway.

Eventually the piano is back together again, although the woman who promised to love, honor and tickle my ivories makes a big point of mentioning that I wound up with a few extra parts. I counter by explaining that 79 keys are more than enough for most songs.

For two years the piano sits in the basement. The 13-year-old becomes a 14-year-old. Then she becomes a 15-year-old. What she does not become, however, is a piano player. This is partly because of arrested outer digital small muscle development. And partly because of a minimal audio-tonal dysfunction. But mainly it is because, in two years, she practices a total of 17 minutes.

Meanwhile, I have been busy putting up walls and ceilings and lights and bars to convert the basement into a rec room, the focal point of which will be the pool table with which my loved ones are going to surprise me on Christmas. To make room for the pool table, the unused piano with the 79 keys is going to have to go.

I mention this to the woman who promised to love, honor and chalk my cue.

"Maybe we can sell it," she says.

"It's going to be pretty tough selling a 79-key piano that's roughly the size of the World Trade Center."

"Well then, we'll give it away. I'm sure there are plenty of churches that would like to have a piano that big."

"There are plenty of churches that would like to *be* that big," I point out. "Anyway, unless you can find a church that has Arnold Schwarzenegger as the choir director, you might as well forget it. There's no way to get that piano out of the basement."

"Can't you just take it apart and then reassemble it, like you did before?"

"Not since I put in that new ceiling. It's so low now by the stairway that the piano won't even go out in sections. I'm afraid that I'm going to have to break it apart and junk it."

"You can't do that," she protests. "This piano's an antique. Just look at the date on that nameplate . . . 1900."

"That's not the year it was made. It's the weight."

The news that I am planning to kill off the piano creates an uproar throughout the house. The 15-year-old argues that I have no right to destroy "her" piano, a position that falls apart when I point out that I have spent roughly 10 times as much effort moving it as she has spent playing it. The 11-year-old accuses me of being a music hater, a charge I find remarkable coming from a kid who owns every album ever made by KISS.

On the day designated for the piano to go to that great concert hall in the sky, I borrow a sledge hammer, carry it downstairs and deliver a mighty smash. It splinters into a dozen pieces. So I borrow another sledge hammer.

For more than three hours I beat on the piano, causing it considerable discomfort, but little measurable damage. If this piano were a Pinto, it would be on fire by now. If it were California, half of it would be floating in the ocean. I don't know who put this piano together, but I sure wish he had built the *Titanic*.

Eventually, however, the piano cracks and then crumbles. In five hours it is reduced to pieces small enough to fit through the basement doorway.

For the next two weeks, however, the 15-year-old glares at me over the dinner table. She will never forgive me, she says, for killing her piano. I have committed murder.

I prefer to think of it as self-defense.

9

That's
my boy?

When our oldest son turns out to be athletic, talented and popular, it comes as something of a surprise to us. We always assumed that he was going to take after me.

By the time he is 11, he is playing quarterback on his PeeWee football team, singing in the Boys Choir and stirring up considerable speculation in the neighborhood as to who his real father is.

Still, it is enjoyable following his activities, especially his football games. Because among my fantasies that are suitable for family viewing is the one where I am sitting in the stands, watching my favorite football team warm up.

Suddenly the coach appears at my side.

"Thank goodness you're here, D. L.," he gasps. "Freddie Throwback, our All-Pro quarterback, just broke his arm. We need you to take his place."

"Me? I've never played quarterback in my life. Why me?"

"Because I can spot a natural athlete in a minute and it's obvious that you're it. It's so obvious from the way you move, the way you sit, the way you eat your hot dog."

"You can do it, darling," the woman at my side murmurs. "You're such a man."

I hurry down to the field. They hand me the ball. I throw it. The Super Bowl is under way. Having never played quarterback before, my success is mixed. In other words, I do not pass for a touchdown on every play. Sometimes I have to run for them.

Which is pretty much the way it happens at a game mid-way through the 11-year-old's season. I am sitting in the stands, watching my favorite team warm up. Suddenly the coach appears at my side.

"Thank goodness you're here, Doyle," he says, "The officials haven't shown up. We need you to take the place of the referee."

"Me? I've never been a referee before. Why me?"

"Because everybody else I asked turned me down."

"You can do it, dummy," the woman at my side snickers. "You've always said that anybody with half a brain could be a football official. You're perfectly qualified."

I hurry down the field. They hand me the whistle. I blow it. The PeeWee football game is under way.

As the kickoff sails through the autumn air, I run through the signals in my mind. Hands on hips means "offsides." Arms rotated in a clockwise roll means "illegal procedure." Standing on the left foot with the right foot hooked behind the left ankle means "tripping." Hopping alternately from one foot to another while bending in a semi-crouched position means "referee forgot to wear important piece of protective equipment."

My thoughts are interrupted by a loud, ugly voice from the stands:

"Hey ref, you stink."

I am jolted by that. I expected to get razzing. But not before I even made a call.

The game gets going. On the second play, I detect premature movement in the offensive line. I throw my first penalty flag. Illegal procedure. As I walk off the five-yard penalty, the same ugly voice booms out from the stands:

"Hey ref, how can you sleep with all this noise?"

The game resumes. The visiting team's quarterback breaks away for a long touchdown run. The ugly voice booms out from the stands:

"Hey ref, you're missing a heck of a game."

I ignore the voice and the game continues. The teams struggle valiantly back and forth, forth and back. The warm afternoon is filled with the clatter of little cleats. Down here on the field you do not merely see the action. You feel it. You smell it. And you hear it.

"You clipped me . . . no I didn't . . . you did, too . . . no I didn't and if you say it again I'll get my brother to punch your face off . . . yeah? well my brother can punch your brother's face off . . ."

The game moves along. I spot an infraction. I reach for my penalty flag, start to throw it, change my mind. I know the signal for clipping. I know the signal for offensive holding. But I do not know the signal for "illegal time out so the left guard can do what he forgot to do at halftime." I decide not to throw the flag. From up in the stands the familiar ugly voice shrieks:

"Hey, ref, too bad you couldn't find a striped shirt for your guide dog."

The game finally ends. It all went remarkably well, except for the leather lung up in the stands who kept insulting me. Next time, I think I'll leave her at home.

When football season ends, the 11-year-old wants to play basketball. But I convince him to join the Rotary Boys Choir. In a choir, he will learn musical skills that will last him a lifetime, I point out. He will need more than athletics to become a well-rounded person, I point out. Besides, I don't know any basketball signals.

The choir season moves along smoothly until June, when the woman who promised to love, honor and ignore my sour notes brings him home from practice with big news.

"The choir's going to New York City for its annual trip," she says.

"Wonderful place, New York City," I say. "Filled with ethnic diversification, cultural opportunities, cosmopolitan excitement . . . "

"They need one more male chaperone."

". . . crime, filth, drugs. It's no place for a sensitive child like ours."

"Don't be absurd," she snaps. "That sensitive child spent all morning trying to dissect a frog."

"So?"

"The frog wasn't dead. Anyway, it's too late to weasel out of it. I've already volunteered you. The choir director says you'll be perfect."

"Because I project the image of a firm, decisive authority figure necessary for leading 50 impressionable young men on a trip like this?"

"Because he knows that if you skip a week of work nobody's going to miss you."

So I agree to spend a week as a chaperone for the Rotary Boys Choir as they travel to Philadelphia, Valley Forge, Gettysburg and New York City.

On the day we are scheduled to leave, I pack, selecting only those things I feel will be absolutely necessary for a week-long trip with 50 boys between the ages of 10 and 18: Underwear, socks, shirts, slacks, pajamas, a shaving kit, a pair of ear plugs, a small bottle of aspirin and a large bottle of Scotch.

"You're not really taking all that stuff?" says the woman who promised to love, honor and sit on my suitcase.

"You're right. I'll leave the pajamas and the shaving kit at home."

That evening we drive to the place where the buses are to pick up the choir. The buses arrive, the suitcases are loaded into the luggage compartments and the choir scrambles aboard. Not surprisingly, there are a few cases of last-minute changes of heart as a vague future adventure becomes a frightening current reality. Some are openly sobbing as they plead with their families to let them stay at home.

But eventually the choir director convinces all of the chaperones to get on the buses and we are on our way: Two buses, eight chaperones, 50 kids and 600 pounds of chocolate chip cookies to tide them over until the first rest stop.

The first part of our trip takes 12 hours. Twelve hours on a Greyhound bus is not the most relaxing way to travel. But it is better than five minutes on a DC-10. Shortly after 8 in the morning we pull into the outskirts of Philadelphia.

For breakfast we go to a fast food hamburger place. Before they eat, the boys stand at their tables and sing their traditional "The Lord Bless You and Keep You." Several of the other diners are not sure how to react to this. But when you're eating breakfast off of paper plates in a fast food hamburger place, a little prayer couldn't hurt.

We spend the day in Philadelphia, visiting Ben Franklin's house, touring Independence Hall, shopping at Newmarket and trying to keep the kids from putting any more cracks in the Liberty Bell.

The next day we stop at Valley Forge, where we see George Washington's headquarters, George Washington's chapel and George Washington's chapel's souvenir shop.

Then we are driving through the West Side of Manhattan, headed for our hotel near Times Square, where we will spend the next three days.

This is, I realize, a whole different ball game. How are we going to herd 50 kids around Manhattan on that crowded, dirty subway system? Where are we going to find restaurants in Manhattan eager to serve 50 active, boisterous kids? And what's going to happen when 50 apple-cheeked young boys from Middle America come into contact with the lowlife of New York? The muggers. The junkies. The prostitutes.

But it's too late to worry about that now. We're here. The muggers, the junkies, the prostitutes are going to have to protect themselves as best they can.

Chaperoning 50 boys around New York City for three days proves to be another learning experience. What I learn is never to do it again. If ever I am tempted to try something like it again, all I have to do is refer to the diary I kept:

TUESDAY—Our hotel is the Edison, an old but serviceable place on 47th Street, in the heart of the theater district. Adjoining the hotel is the Edison Theater. Directly across the street is the New Orleans Off-Broadway movie theater. The Edison is presenting *Oh, Calcutta!* The New Orleans is showing a triple feature: *Johnny Wadd, Superstar, Teeny Buns* and *Maiden Head.* I wonder if they have group rates?

In the evening we went to Radio City Music Hall to see the show. It was outstanding, with all sorts of music, dancing and stage effects. The kids were clearly impressed. An alto named Cedric, who's about 14, even asked me if I thought we could go backstage.

"You want to get a closer look at all that stage equipment?" I asked him.

"I want to get a closer look at those Rockettes."

WEDNESDAY—We spent the morning taking a Gray Line tour of lower Manhattan, including Chinatown, the Battery and the World Trade Center. Our guide was a dapper gent from Hungary who said he speaks 11 languages. When we were getting on the bus, he asked me where the group was from.

"Dayton, Ohio," I told him.

"What kind of a town is it?"

"Well, it's a nice place to live, but you wouldn't want to visit there," I said.

"Don't feel bad," he said. "Everything outside of New York City is Dayton."

New Yorkers have a real peculiar view of the rest of the country. Probably comes from sitting around in blackouts wondering if the rest of the country will pay their bills for them.

At the World Trade Center, which is a pretty fair-sized set of buildings, our guide pointed out that it serves 80,000 visitors a day.

Cedric is awed.

"Gosh," he said. "Imagine how many girls must be in there."

After the World Trade Center, where the main topic of conversation was "what would happen if you threw your camera from the 110th-floor observation deck and it landed on top of a person's head," we went to the United Nations. Cedric tried to pick up a girl in the coffee shop. She looked Spanish, so he tried to strike up a conversation in Spanish. Unfortunately, the girl couldn't speak Spanish. Then again, neither could Cedric.

We had dinner at a place called the Ruc Restaurant, a Czechoslovakian spot on East 72nd. To get there we had to buy three subway tokens for each person in the group. The guy in the subway token booth was not real thrilled when I walked up and told him I needed 174 tokens. He gave me so much lip that I was tempted to let him have the pleasure of having all 50 kids come up to his booth one at a time to buy their tokens. With money they've been carrying in their pockets all day. Next to their chocolate bars.

The Ruc is a nice place with a garden dining area. From our table we had a lovely view of a second floor loft where a yoga class was exercising in front of a large, uncovered window. No dinner is complete without a view of exercises being done by a fat lady. Wearing pink leotards. Who doesn't shave under her arms.

The menu at the Ruc included four types of goulash, veal shank, chicken paprika and calves brains with eggs. Not one kid in our group ordered calves brains with eggs.

THURSDAY—For our trip to the Staten Island Ferry, I had to buy 58 more subway tokens. Of which 57 wound up being used. "I saved mine," said a tiny blond soprano.

"Then, how did you get through the turnstile?" I asked him.

"I walked under," he said. "I've been doing that all week long."

There's a lot of crime on New York's subways.

The Staten Island Ferry ride was great. As we glided past the Statue of Liberty, we all rushed to the starboard side for a good look at the glorious green beacon of opportunity to countless huddled masses yearning to breathe free. All except one alto, who seized that opportunity to rush to the boat's snack bar now that it was deserted. As we passed the famous symbol of liberty, he sat with his back to the rail, munching a Hershey bar and spilling orange drink on his shirt.

After dinner at Mamma Leone's, some of the older boys had a chance to walk around Times Square on their own. For them it was probably pretty exciting. But, for those of us who remember how it used to be, the deterioration of the area is sad and depressing. There are so many drug pushers on 42nd Street these days that you can hardly get into the dirty bookstores.

FRIDAY—Shortly after 9 a.m. we boarded our homeward-bound buses in front of the New Orleans Off-Broadway theater. It was sort of a shame to leave without having a chance to see the new triple feature: *Pastries, Candy Girls* and *Love Is Not Enough.*

As we pulled through the intersection of 47th and Eighth Avenue, I noticed that Cedric was sitting across the aisle from me, writing on some postcards.

"Who are you writing to?" I asked.

"A couple of girls back home," he said.

I don't know why I bothered to ask.

Fortunately, at the age of 12, our soprano has not yet discovered sex. Unfortunately, he has discovered politics. We learn this shameful truth one evening at the dinner table when he announces that he is going to run for office on his junior high student council.

"That's wonderful," says the woman who promised to love, honor and stuff my ballot box.

"I don't know," I caution. "I mean, sure, you've got a lot of political assets: A warm grin, a plaid shirt, a brother who acts like a three-year-old, a white-haired mother with a sharp tongue. But what about your qualifications?"

"Qualifications?"

"Sure. To hold office, you have to be honest, intelligent, courageous and unselfish with your time and efforts."

"You do?"

"Well, I suppose, three out of four wouldn't be bad."

"You don't even know what you're talking about," says the 15-year-old, looking up from her plate, where she has arranged her macaroni and cheese into the shape of John Travolta. It is not the first time she has said this to me. In fact, I have noticed that the older she gets, the less I know what I'm talking about.

"You mean you don't need qualifications to run for junior high student council?" I ask.

"Of course you do. You need to be cool, have sharp clothes, good records and feathered hair."

Having delivered this piece of political insight, she leaves the table and heads for her bedroom, which is her way of saying that she has no more time to waste in idle conversation with persons in advanced stages of premature senility.

We turn our attention back to the 12-year-old.

"What office do you plan to run for?" I ask.

"Vice president."

"Vice president? Why not president?"

"Because," he says, "the president has to do all the work. If you're vice president, you get to just sit around and suck up the glory."

"You mean like George Bush?"

"Who?"

"Never mind. Tell me, who else is running for vice president?"

"There's one girl and one boy. Which is sort of bad, because some of the boys will vote for me and some will vote for him, but all the girls probably will vote for her."

"Bloc voting. That could be a problem."

"Yeah, but some of my buddies are going to help me."

"How?"

"They're going to break into her locker and get a look at her campaign plans."

"Uh, I think you'd better deep-six that idea," I suggest.

"Why?"

"Trust me. Anyway, what about your campaign? Have you thought about a platform? Posters? A slogan?"

"Sure, I already got a slogan."

"Great. Let's hear it."

"It's 'Vote for me or I'll punch your face off.'"

"Well, that does have a certain ring to it," I admit. "But, if you don't mind a little advice, it sounds a bit negative. Don't you think you should try a more positive approach?"

"Yeah, maybe," he agrees. "How about, 'A vote for me is a vote for not getting your face punched off.'"

By now, I suspect that the kid isn't really running for junior high student council, he is running for dictator of a South American banana republic. Still, I don't want to discourage his political ambitions. If the parents of earlier generations had discouraged their young candidates, there's no telling what kind of political incompetents would be running the country today.

Besides, if he keeps going, who knows? Maybe some day I'll be the First Father.

10
The price
is wrong

As they come from the factory, kids generally are not all that expensive to keep running. Baby clothes are cheap, toys don't cost much and a jar of strained apricots can last a week.

But after they get a few miles on them, you have to take them back to the shop more and more often for repairs. In our case, three of them have been recalled because of vision problems.

I blame that on the woman who promised to love, honor and be the apple of my eye. I have 20-20 vision, but she has exceptionally poor eyesight. Which may or may not help explain why she agreed to go out with me in the first place. When she accepted my invitation for a date, I assumed she was overlooking my flaws. As it turns out, she just couldn't see them.

As we continued to date, a lot of our courtship was spent on her living room floor. Looking for contact lenses. Eventually, we decided to get married, and I gave her a diamond ring.

"What is it?" she asked.

"It's a diamond," I said.

She squinted down at the quarter-carat stone.

"I'll take your word for it," she said.

After we got married, I was aware that our kids might inherit some of her characteristics, including her poor eyesight. But I also assumed they would inherit some of my characteristics, including my good eyesight. The way I figured it, half of our kids would be bright and attractive, and the other half would take after me.

Which is not the way it always turns out, as I discover one evening when the first kid is about seven years old.

"I think the first kid needs glasses," she says.

"What makes you think so?"

"I noticed when she was watching cartoons the other day she sat with her nose practically touching the screen."

"That doesn't necessarily mean anything. Lots of kids sit too close to the television."

"We were at the movies."

Three weeks, eight fittings and a couple of dozen bills later, the seven-year-old is wearing glasses. If wearing glasses bothers her, she doesn't mention it. Not, at least, until she turns 14 and announces that she wants contact lenses.

"I don't really think you're old enough for contact lenses," I point out. "They're sort of expensive, they're a lot of trouble and you probably would have a hard time getting adjusted to them."

"I'll pay for them myself, and I'll take real good care of them," she pleads.

"Sorry, I've made up my mind. There's no sense debating."

"All right," she wails, "but don't blame me when you find tire tracks in your tomato plants."

"Tire tracks? What are you talking about? What the heck do tire tracks in my tomato plants have to do with you not getting contact lenses?"

"It's pretty obvious that no cool boys are going to be interested in me as long as I'm wearing these goony glasses. So I'll have to start hanging around bars and pool rooms until I find somebody willing to take me out, and he'll probably belong to a motorcycle gang, and some night when he brings me home he'll drive his chopper through the backyard and do wheelies in your tomato boxes and then . . ."

"Oh, for heaven's sake, go ahead and get the contact lenses." I think she had the same debating teacher her mother did.

The second kid gets his glasses when he is 11, following reports from school that his teachers think he is having trouble seeing the blackboard from his seat. Which is in the front row.

He is not happy about the glasses.

"If I wear glasses, I won't be able to play football when I get to high school," he points out.

"If you don't wear glasses, you'll never get to high school," I point out.

A year later he announces that he, too, wants contact lenses.

"I think you're too young for contact lenses," I say. "Let's wait a while."

"All right. But don't blame me when you find flashbulbs in your tomatoes."

"Flashbulbs? What do flashbulbs in my tomatoes have to do with you not getting contact lenses?"

"Simple. If I have to keep wearing glasses, kids will start calling me four-eyes, and that'll make me grow up maladjusted, and I'll probably become a psychotic adult who goes berserk some night and goes on a murder spree with a chain saw, and the *National Enquirer* will be sending photographers to sneak around and take pictures of the house where I grew up, and they'll be walking through your tomato boxes, dropping their flashbulbs and snapping . . ."

"Never mind. Just get the contact lenses."

The youngest kid gets his glasses when he is just four. Not only does he have to wear glasses, he also has to wear a patch over one eye for part of each day. Which makes him easy to spot. He's the only kid in nursery school who looks like Moshe Dayan.

But so far he hasn't asked for contact lenses. In a way, I'm looking forward to it. I can't wait to hear what kinds of terrible things are in store for my tomato plants.

The only one of our kids who doesn't wear contact lenses or glasses is the seven-year-old. But he's the one who is accident-prone.

Every family has one kid who can fall out of a church pew and break his leg, cut himself with a spoon or get a concussion playing Monopoly.

Fortunately, years of fatherhood have prepared me to cope with almost any emergency. Whenever the seven-year-old makes another attempt at self-destruction, I turn to one of the other kids and say in a cool, calm voice: "Go get your mother."

Unfortunately, his mother is not always there. Which is the case on the afternoon he does a perfect one-and-a-half backward dive off the kitchen counter. It happens at lunchtime. As I am walking into the kitchen, I see him standing on the counter, looking into the cupboard for something to eat. He's probably hunting for the peanut butter, which, as a result of its price, we have begun hiding. Behind the caviar.

Suddenly his foot slips and he topples backward off the counter, landing on the kitchen floor and striking his head against the leg of the new chopping block I just bought for myself.

Quickly, I rush across the kitchen and bend over for a hasty examination. I breathe a sigh of relief when I discover that there does not seem to be much damage. It is made of good, solid wood.

The seven-year-old, on the other hand, is yelling his head off.

"Where does it hurt?" I ask.

He continues yelling.

"Stop crying and tell me where it hurts," I demand. That's a phrase I learned from my mother when I was little. Actually, it's a variation of a phrase I learned from my mother when I was little. The original phrase was, "Stop crying this instant or I'll give you something to really cry about."

The seven-year-old continues his imitation of an air-raid siren.

I lean down to get a closer look. It is like sticking your head under the hood of a car whose horn is stuck. My only consolation is that, if he's seriously hurt, there will be no need to call the hospital. They can hear him yelling from here to the Mayo Clinic.

My medical knowledge is somewhat limited, but I have been reading up on CPR, artificial respiration and the Heimlich maneuver. Unfortunately, I don't see any way to apply any of that to the kid's current injury, which is a cut on the back of his head.

The only thing I know about bleeding is that the best way to stop it is to apply a tourniquet. While I still am trying to figure a way to get a tourniquet around the seven-year-old's head, the 12-year-old walks into the kitchen. He notices his brother yelling.

"Something wrong with him?" he asks.

"He fell and hurt himself."

"Oh, he's such a baby. I'll bet he's not even hurt."

"If he's not hurt, how come all this blood is coming out of the back of his head?"

"He's just doing that to get attention."

The 12-year-old and the seven-year-old never have been particularly close.

The 15-year-old follows the 12-year-old into the kitchen. She looks at her brother lying on the kitchen floor, blood dripping from the cut on his head. She bends down for a closer look. She turns to me, a worried look on her face.

"Does this mean lunch is going to be late?" she asks.

"How can you think of lunch?" I demand. "Your brother is hurt, and I'm not sure how to take care of it. What's the first thing your mother would do in this situation?"

"Pass out," says the 15-year-old. "She can't stand the sight of blood."

Instead, I clean the wound, apply some ice, give him some baby aspirin and tell him to lie down. After an hour or so, he stops crying.

"Feel better now?" I ask.

"Uh-huh," he says. "But I'm hungry. Can I have a peanut butter sandwich?"

"Sure. I'll make it for you."

"That's OK, Dad, I'll do it," he says, jumping off the couch and scrambling up onto the kitchen counter.

The seven-year-old is a real resilient kid. He's going to be eight pretty soon. Maybe.

In spite of all his accidents, he has never had a tooth knocked out. Which comes as little consolation to my wallet. Because what the dentist doesn't get, the tooth fairy will.

In 15 years of fatherhood, I figure I have covered enough debts for the tooth fairy to pay for a nice piece of land. In the center of Manhattan.

The seven-year-old started dropping bicuspids about a year ago, and it's beginning to look as if he's going to make a career of it.

"You know," I mention to the woman who promised to love, honor and iron my floss, "this whole tooth fairy business is getting a little out of control. And it's really silly, if you think about it. I mean, losing teeth is just a normal part of growing up, so why do we have to pay them for it? We don't reward them for outgrowing their shoes."

"I know," she says, "but it's a harmless little custom that makes kids happy."

"Harmless? Are you kidding? A kid loses a tooth, we give him money, and what does he do with it? He goes out and spends it on bubble gum so he can lose more teeth. It's like giving the 15-year-old a chocolate bar every time she grows a new zit."

"Well, I have to admit, I'm getting a little tired of paying him so often. Do you know I've had to write him three checks this week alone?"

"That's another thing. Where is he getting all those teeth? He's had one under his pillow practically every night for the past month, but he's only got two gaps in his mouth. There must be a pusher hanging around the schoolyard selling hot incisors."

"I've been wondering about that myself," she agrees. "I think we should keep a sharp eye on the dog for a while. If she starts skipping the meat and goes right for the apple sauce at dinner time, we may have our answer."

"Well, I think it's gotten out of hand, and I say we stop paying."

"I know what you mean. But I think you're making too much of a fuss over an occasional dollar."

"Dollar? I thought it was a quarter."

"That was three kids ago. Inflation is everywhere."

"That does it. It's absolutely ridiculous for us to be paying that kind of money every time he loses a tooth. There's no reason why we should have to pay extortion to a second grader just because of some stupid myth. It's time he learned what life is really like. So go in there and tell him."

"If you want him to learn what life is all about, you go in and tell him. Of course, if you tell him there's no tooth fairy, he'll probably start to wonder about the Easter Bunny and Santa Claus, too. Which means his faith in all the things we have told him will start to disappear and probably carry over into his developing years, causing a total lack of trust in all of our institutions, and by the time he's in college he'll undoubtedly become a campus radical with long hair and sandals, and he'll advocate the violent overthrow of the government, and your name will wind up in the history books as the father of an anarchist. Karl Marx's father probably refused to put any pfennings under his pillow."

I walk into the kid's room and slip two bucks under his pillow. But if I ever run into the guy who started this tooth fairy thing, I think I'll knock his teeth out.

The tooth fairy isn't the only one who has been affected by inflation, I suppose. But it's hard for me to get interested in economics that I can't see. Lots of people can sit around for hours wondering how the President's import policy will affect the Gross National Product. I, on the other hand, spend most of my time wondering how a 15-year-old's $40 Nikes can wear out when they spend most of their time sitting in the middle of the living room floor. Not only do I not know how to get ahead in the stock market, I have a great deal of trouble finding a parking spot at the supermarket. My most complicated financial problem is trying to decide which line at the bank will move fastest.

But it doesn't do any good to ignore inflation, because eventually it will come looking for you. One time it even is brought into the living room by the 12-year-old.

"Dad," he begins, "can I talk to you?"

"Certainly."

"It's about my allowance."

"That's all right, son, no need to thank me. I'm happy to give it to you."

"Well, that's not why I wanted to talk to you. What I wanted to say is that it's not enough. I need a raise."

"A raise? How much are you getting now?"

"Three dollars a week."

"That certainly seems like it should be enough for a boy your age."

"You can't be serious. When the guys at school found out I was only getting $3 a week, they said I should apply for food stamps."

"My boy, when I was your age I got 35 cents a week. And that had to take care of all my expenses, including the Saturday afternoon movie."

"Mom says they didn't have movies when you were my age."

"Don't listen to her. Sometimes Mom says things she really doesn't mean, especially when she's tired. It's a lot of work standing in front of a mirror all day trying to pull out the gray hairs."

"I don't know anything about that. All I know is that it's just about impossible to get by on $3 a week these days. Like, if I wanted to take a girl roller skating, it would take me two weeks to save up for it. And that's not counting taking her somewhere to eat afterwards."

"Dating can be expensive," I agree. "It would be a lot easier if you learned to be a gigolo."

"What's a gigolo?"

"That's a guy who hangs around with rich widows and lets them pay for everything."

"There aren't a whole lot of rich widows at my junior high," he says.

"I suppose not. Well, if I agree to a raise, how much do you need?"

"At least a couple of bucks."

"That's an awful big increase," I point out. I start to tell him about inflation and wage freezes and negative economic indicators and all the other things that the boss tells me whenever I ask for a raise. But it occurs to me that a 12-year-old boy is not likely to be knowledgeable about such matters. I will have to explain it to him in terms that he can comprehend.

"OK, son, let me try to make you understand my problem. First of all, you've got to picture Dad's salary as if it were a pie. Or, maybe, a pizza."

"What kind?"

"Small and plain. Now then, if this pizza is divided into eight equal slices and then you take each slice and . . ."

"Dad," he interrupts, "I don't know where you're headed with all this pizza business, but let me try to make you understand my problem: "In January of 1983, the cost of living index rose 1.4 percent. Computed on an annual basis, this would imply a 16.8 percent increase in the cost of living. This, however, fails to take into account the fact that the increase would be calculated on a compound basis, giving us in actuality an 18.1 percent cost of living increase. Now, if you will remember that my allowance in the past fiscal year failed to increase at all and add to that the predicted inflationary trend as noted in the latest financial projections of some government economists . . ."

"All right, all right, you can have the two bucks."

I don't know where the kid learns that stuff. All I know is that the next time I try for a raise, I'm sending him in to talk to the boss.

There are a lot of things like that they don't tell you about being a father.

I knew, of course, about 4 a.m. feedings. But nobody bothered to warn me that what goes down doesn't necessarily stay down. I knew that even the best-trained toddler occasionally will have an accident in bed. But I didn't know it would be my bed.

And I knew that when they got older they would get involved in activities that required frequent fund raisers. But I never realized who the frequent fund raisers were.

Fatherhood is not an experience; it is an 18-year paper drive. Show me a father who is not up to his knees in soapy water at a Saturday morning YMCA car wash and I'll show you a father who probably is out delivering brownies for the bake sale.

The strange thing is, I do not know of any father who ever actually volunteered to do these things. Usually it works the way it happens to me when I come home from work one afternoon.

"Saturday probably would be a good day for it," says the woman who promised to love, honor and raise my hand.

"It?"

"To help out on the fund raiser."

"What are we raising funds for this time? New shin guards for the

15-year-old's soccer team? Drip-dry sleeping bags for the seven-year-old's Cub Scout Den?"

"The 12-year-old's choir is trying to raise money for a trip to Germany next year. It would be a great cultural event for them. A real learning experience."

"I can just see them scribbling graffiti on the Berlin Wall," I agree. "So, what do I have to do?"

"Sell a few raffle tickets."

"Now wait a minute. I'll load old newspapers into the back of a truck, and I'll wash cars in the middle of November. I'll even try to lift your brownies and deliver them to the bake sale. But I'll be darned if I'm going to try to put the bite on people for a raffle ticket I know they don't want."

"You're probably right," she says. "I won't argue with you."

"You won't?"

"No. Why should you have to go out and sell four or five raffle tickets just so your oldest son can spend two weeks in the land of Beethoven and Bach and Wagner when he could stay right here at home and spend all his time in his bedroom listening to his stereo on full blast playing to Ozzie Osbourne albums and . . ."

"Where are the raffle tickets?"

"In your desk drawer."

"By the way," I ask, "what are they raffling off?"

"It's a terrific deal. For $100 they get a prime rib dinner with wine, plus a chance on a new Buick, a television, a . . ."

"Wait a minute. What was that?"

"A prime rib dinner with wine, a . . ."

"I mean that first number."

"Oh. The tickets are $100."

"Where in the heck am I supposed to find someone with $100 to shell out for a raffle ticket?"

"It shouldn't be that hard. We must know some people who have a lot of money."

"Only our pediatrician. And by the time we get through to his office, that Buick will be six years old."

"Well, how about the people at your office?"

"You're not serious. Newspaper people wouldn't buy a 50-cent ticket on the Hope diamond. Think about it. What would you do if I came home from work and said I'd just bought a $100 raffle ticket?"

"Break every bone in your head."

"Exactly."

Still, there's no harm in trying. On Monday morning I check around the office to see if any of my co-workers is interested in buying a $100 raffle ticket. Eight of my co-workers say no. Eleven of my co-workers say hell, no. Twenty-three of my co-workers remind me that I never bought any of their kids' Girl Scout cookies.

In three weeks, I have sold enough $100 raffle tickets to send my 12-year-old son on a trip to Steubenville, Ohio. I'm still hoping I'll be able to sell some to friends. But the odds are against it.

A man with $100 raffle tickets to sell has no friends.

11

A man for all seasons

Fathers always get the dirty jobs on holidays.

On Christmas, it's the father's job to make the 12-foot tree fit into the eight-foot living room.

On the Fourth of July, it's the father's job to hold the match to the Roman candle that has a quarter-inch of fuse and enough powder in it to blow up a subcontinent.

On Halloween, it's the father's job to reach his hand down into the pumpkin and scoop out all that cold, stringy stuff.

And on Easter, it's the father's job to hide the eggs.

I'm not sure why this is. It may have socio-religious connotations. Perhaps it's a historical carryover from the days when Easter egg hiding was a difficult and dangerous job. Or it may just be that mothers have always been smarter than fathers.

Whatever the reason, I'm always the one who has to find a dozen new hiding places in the same rooms where I've been hiding Easter eggs from the same kids all their lives.

"Why do I have to be the one to do this all the time?" I ask the woman who promised to love, honor and hop with me down the bunny trail of life.

"Because it's one of the few things you do well," she says. "Although, if you don't mind, I'd just as soon you didn't hide any of them in the bathroom again like you did last year."

"Hey, how was I supposed to know that would be the morning the four-year-old would remember to flush?"

While she fills their baskets with cellophane grass, jelly beans and enough candy to keep our dentist in Hawaiian vacations for the rest of his life, I look for places in the kitchen and family room to hide the eggs that the kids have dyed.

Hiding the eggs is not the only problem. It's almost as tough explaining to them why the eggs that were on the kitchen table when they went to bed are scattered all over two rooms when they get up the next morning. Our story is that the Easter bunny hops in after we are all asleep, fills their baskets with candy and then hides their eggs. They've always bought that story, but I'm not sure how long it's going to last. The 15-year-old is starting to get suspicious.

I hide the eggs.

Hiding the four-year-old's eggs is not much of a challenge. But then, how hard can it be to hide something from a kid who can never find his shoes, his toothbrush, his napkin or his bedroom?

Hiding the 15-year-old's eggs, on the other hand, is a real test of skill. She can find anything, no matter how well hidden. Especially if her mother just bought it and it goes with the slacks she's planning to wear to school tomorrow.

It takes me about two hours to hide the eggs. I hide them under ash trays. In the bottom of the cookie jar. On top of a lamp. Underneath chairs. On Easter morning, the kids get up and hunt for their eggs.

The four-year-old quickly finds all of his, even though I have cleverly hidden them in the middle of the kitchen floor. The 15-year-old finds hers in one of the 30-second intervals between incoming phone calls. The 12-year-old has a bit more trouble, but eventually he finds all of his. Including the ones I have hidden in the dog's water bowl, in the bottom of his Easter basket and in the egg carton in the refrigerator.

After an hour of hunting, however, the seven-year-old still hasn't found his last Easter egg.

"Maybe I was too tough with that one," I whisper to the woman who promised to love, honor and tell me if I was getting hotter or colder. "It's in a place he'll probably never think of looking."

"Where's that?" she asks.

"In the soap dish."

Like Easter, Halloween somehow has become "my" holiday. Each year I'm the one who is expected to go out with the kids and find pumpkins to carve. It's a heavy responsibility. Some years I am barely equal to the task.

On the second weekend of this past October, for instance, the woman who promised to love, honor and light my candle asks me when I am going to take the kids out to get their pumpkins.

"Relax," I say. "It's only the second weekend of the month. There's plenty of time."

On the third weekend of this past October, she asks again.

"It's still too early," I point out. "If we buy the pumpkins now, they'll want to carve them right away. And by Halloween, our jack o' lanterns will have faces like Gabby Hayes."

On the fourth weekend of this past October, I glance at the calendar and notice that it is just three days until Halloween.

"Why didn't you remind me?" I snap as I herd the kids into the car.

We drive to the little country store where each year we buy our Halloween pumpkins.

"Hi," I say to the lady there, "we need four pumpkins."

"All out," she says.

"All out where?"

"I mean, we don't have any. It's almost Halloween, you know."

"I know, I know."

We get back into the car.

"Don't worry," I assure the group in the backseat. "There's another little country place about a mile down the road. I'm sure they'll have plenty. Ol' dad won't let you down."

"Jeff Hatton's dad bought their pumpkins two weeks ago," the seven-year-old says.

We drive a mile down the road.

"Hi," I say to the guy there, "we need four pumpkins."

"Only got one left."

"Well, usually we get one for each kid. But I suppose we could get one for the whole family if it's big enough. Is it very big?"

"See for yourself," he says, pointing to something in the corner of the room. It is the world's biggest pumpkin. Either that, or somebody has painted the Goodyear blimp orange.

"You want it?" he asks.

"Not unless it comes with six white mice and a magic wand."

We get back into the car.

"Don't worry," I assure the group in the backseat, "there's another little country place just across the state line."

"Jeff Hatton's dad carved their pumpkins last weekend and there's one in every room in their house," the seven-year-old says. I'm getting a little tired of the seven-year-old. And I'm not too wild about Jeff Hatton's dad, either.

Five little country places and 53 miles down the road later, we still have not found any pumpkins. The group in the backseat is starting to look a lot like a mob. The four-year-old is sniffling. The seven-year-old is talking about how Jeff Hatton's dad grew each one of their pumpkins personally on days when he wasn't otherwise occupied in taking his son to the circus, inventing baseball or defeating the Nazis at the Battle of the Bulge. The 12-year-old and the 15-year-old are discussing ways to sneak into an orphanage.

I decide to give up on the little county store routine and try a big city supermarket. We stop at the first supermarket we can find.

"Do you have any pumpkins?" I ask the kid in the produce department.

"No. But we got some real nice bananas."

"Terrific. We can be the only family on the block with a lighted banana in the window."

We try another supermarket.

"Sure, we've got pumpkins," the produce manager says. "Of course, this close to Halloween, they're not all real attractive."

We check out the pumpkins that the store manager has described as "not real attractive." I can't be sure, but my guess is that he is the kind of man who would describe the Boston Strangler as "not real friendly." Not only are these pumpkins not real attractive, they are painfully homely. They are the kind of pumpkins that stayed home on prom night, with their hair in rollers and their faces covered with Clearasil.

But, at this point, we are in no position to hold out for Bo Derek. We buy four pumpkins and head for the cash register. On the way, we pass through the meat department. The cases, I notice, are piled high with turkeys.

For just a second I hesitate. But heck, I tell myself, that's almost a month away. Relax, there's plenty of time.

Besides, the Thanksgiving turkey is not my assignment. We always spend Thanksgiving at grandmother's house.

I don't know who it was that wrote about the joy of traveling "over the river and through the woods, to grandmother's house we go." But I'm willing to bet my last Currier and Ives print that he (A) didn't have four kids; (B) never did it more than once; or (C) lied about other things, too.

Then again, maybe his mother-in-law didn't live in an apartment in Cleveland that has just one bedroom. And, even more importantly, just one bathroom.

But, in spite of this, every year we pack the car and drive to Cleveland to spend Thanksgiving with my mother-in-law. We do this even though I do not recall my mother-in-law ever actually inviting us to visit her.

"Of course she wants us to visit her," says the woman who promised to love, honor and break my wishbone. "She loves to see her grandchildren. Don't you remember how emotional she got last year?"

"Sure I do. But I always thought a grandmother was supposed to cry when the kids were leaving, not when they were arriving."

But it is over the Interstate and through the radar traps, to grandmother's house we go. It is shortly after dark when we arrive. Obviously grandmother did not expect us this soon. She is still there.

By the time we unload the car, it is time for bed. In grandmother's apartment there are two twin beds and a couch. Unfortunately, there are seven of us. Not counting the turkey. Which means that four of us have to sleep on the floor. When we all are bedded down in the hallway, the living room, the kitchen and the bathroom, it looks like a scene from one of those documentaries on the housing shortage in Moscow.

For three days we stay in grandmother's one-bedroom, one-bathroom apartment.

On Thanksgiving Day, we watch parades on television, eat turkey that is freshly roasted and spend hours playing board games.

On the day after Thanksgiving, we watch soap operas on television, eat turkey that is warmed up and spend hours playing card games.

On the second day after Thanksgiving, we watch football games on television, eat turkey that is becoming petrified and spend hours looking for the key to grandmother's liquor cabinet.

On the third day after Thanksgiving, we head for home. Thanksgiving weekend at grandmother's house is over. But we'll go back again next year. Next year it's my turn to get the couch.

But there's one holiday tradition that hits me harder than grandmother's floor. It is a tradition that starts one Christmas Eve when our first-born is just four years old. And what makes it worse is that I inflicted it upon myself.

"What are you going to leave for Santa tonight?" I ask her on that Christmas Eve so long ago.

"What do you mean, dearest Daddy?" she asks. She always was a sweet child.

"Well, if Santa is going to be out all night delivering presents to good little girls and boys, he's probably going to get very hungry, don't you think? And thirsty, too. I'll bet he would be awfully happy to find some cookies and hot chocolate waiting for him when he slides down the chimney."

"But, Daddy, we don't have a chimney," she says. She always was a bright kid.

"Let's forget about the chimney part. But, how about the cookies and hot chocolate?"

"The way I look at it, Pops," she says, "if every one of us kids leaves hot chocolate and cookies for him to eat, halfway through the night he's gonna get sick as a dog and he'll have to drive that sleigh with his head hanging over the side." She always was an argumentative little brat. Comes from her mother's side.

Despite her reasoning, it is decided to leave hot chocolate and cookies under the tree that year. Later, after she is in bed, we lay out a mountain of presents under the tree, drink a Christmas toddy or two and prepare to turn in.

"Wait a minute," says the woman who promised to love, honor and throw up the sash, "what about the hot chocolate and cookies?"

"Oh yeah, good thing you reminded me. I'll get rid of them."

"What are you going to do with them?"

"Pour the hot chocolate down the drain and put the cookies back in the cookie jar."

"You can't put those cookies back. What if she sees them in the morning? It would ruin her Christmas."

"You're right. I'll throw the cookies in the garbage back under the sink."

"She still might find them there."

"I could hide them on the top shelf in the closet."

"No good."

Tuck them under the front seat of my car?"

"Nope."

"Bury them in the backyard?"

"No."

"Well, then, how about if I stick their feet in cement and throw them into the East River?"

"Very funny. But the answer is simple, really. All you have to do is eat them. And be sure to leave a few crumbs on the floor, like you usually do."

"But, I don't like cookies. Especially not on top of a fifth of Christmas toddy and a bowl of French onion chip dip."

Naturally, however, I wind up eating the cookies, which I wash down with the hot chocolate, all the time resolving that when the subject comes up next year I will mention that what Santa really likes is a six-pack of Budweiser and a couple of bags of beer nuts.

Thus begins a holiday tradition. Each year, treats are laid out for Santa Claus. Each year, I am expected to dispose of them. In succeeding years I am treated to cookies and milk. Cookies and Coke. Cookies and club soda. Cookies and coffee. Cookies and tea. Cookies and runny Jell-O.

But last Christmas tradition takes a turn for the worse, when the job of selecting the Christmas Eve menu falls to the current four-year-old. It is a job he carries out with great seriousness.

Carefully, he pours a small glass of eggnog into a paper Christmas cup. Then he goes to the cookie jar and selects three Christmas cookies, freshly made by his sister the night before. One is a star. One is a Christmas tree. The third is a camel. Or an armadillo with rickets. It's hard to tell.

When the cookies and the eggnog are under the tree, the four-year-old returns to the refrigerator.

"What are you looking for?" I ask.

"Carrots."

"Carrots?"

"For Santa's reindeer."

This is an unexpected development. None of the others ever considered Santa's reindeer. They were content merely to contribute to Santa's cholesterol buildup, with never a thought for the poor shivering animals up on the rooftop going click, click, click. But this four-year-old has heart. That's nice. Besides, I like carrots.

After a few minutes of browsing through the refrigerator, the four-year-old returns. He is not carrying a carrot. He is carrying an armful of carrots.

"Wait a minute," I say. "What are all those for?"

"One carrot for each reindeer. He has eight, you know. Plus Rudolph."

He spreads out the carrots in front of the tree, next to the Christmas cookies and eggnog. Then he goes to bed, where visions of sugar plums and $49.95 computer games will dance in his head.

Hopefully, I look at the woman who promised to love, honor and see to it that I always get my recommended daily allowance of Vitamin A.

"I'll get the salt," she says.

So I eat the cookie that is shaped like a star and the cookie that is shaped like a Christmas tree and the cookie that is shaped like an armadillo with rickets. And I drink the eggnog. And I eat the carrots. Every darn one of them.

It could be worse, I tell myself. And it probably will be. Because on Christmas afternoon, the four-year-old's big brother asks him why he didn't leave any cookies under the tree for Santa to take back to his elves at the North Pole.

"I forgot," admits the four-year-old. "But I'll do it next year. I'll leave a cookie for each one. Anyways, how many elves are there?"

"Oh," says his brother, "about a thousand."

12

The bad news Stewarts

If there was one part of fatherhood I looked forward to, it was watching my kids participate in sports. Of course, I had no way of knowing about Little League.

They didn't have Little League where I grew up. Where I grew up, organized baseball started when you were 12, beginning with Class F. Class F baseball was not so much a game as it was a test of courage. Those who finished the season could boast to their peers that, "Now I am a man." It was sort of a bar mitzvah in cleats.

Unlike Little League, Class F wasn't run by parents. Which is not to say it didn't have its negative aspects. Probably the most negative of which was that no one wore helmets. Each time we went to the plate, our heads were protected by nothing but the thickness of our flat-tops.

To make matters worse, the pitchers in Class F always were the biggest, strongest kids on the team, huge, hulking brutes. In retrospect, I suppose it was my imagination that made 12-year-olds look like huge, hulking brutes. Then again, it might have been the way they combed their beards.

In any event, Class F baseball was a terrifying experience for me, an ordeal to be survived, nine innings of anguish every Saturday morning. Lord only knows how bad it might have been if I'd actually gotten into a game.

Fortunately, kids' baseball is different now. Games are supervised. They are played on well-groomed fields. Batters wear protective helmets. Just about the only way for a Little League player to get hurt is if he gets caught in the crossfire between parents.

Even so, you don't just jump into Little League. You have to work your way up to it, starting at the age of six in something called T-ball.

I personally feel that the nearest a six-year-old should come to any form of organized baseball is a once-a-year visit to his nearest major league park, where he can drink pop, make lots of trips to the bathroom and fall asleep just before the seventh-inning stretch.

In fact, I say exactly that to the woman who promised to love, honor and wash my resin bag when she mentions that we have a six-year-old who wants to sign up for T-ball.

"But all of his friends are going to be playing," she says.

"So? Why should we bow to peer pressure? There's no time like the present to instill in him a sense of individuality."

"Why? I'll tell you why. Because while all of his little friends are off playing T-ball, he'll be home with nobody to play with. Which means he'll be standing in the kitchen complaining all evening that he has nothing to do. Which means I will start taking extended evening shopping trips. Alone. Which means that you will have to take him with you when you play tennis in your league on . . ."

I drive him to his first T-ball game the following week. When we get to the field, I take him to report to the coach.

"Hi," I say, "this is my son and . . ."

"First things first," the coach says. "Have you signed up for the team photo?"

"Well, no, I . . ."

"That will be $2.75. Just fill out this form."

I fill out a form saying that I will be happy to pay $2.75 for a full-color photo of my son and 14 other sets of skinny legs sticking out from underneath enormous baseball caps. Then I find a seat along the third-base line.

For those who haven't seen it, T-ball is what baseball would be like if Ralph Nader invented it. It has every safety feature short of seat belts on the benches. The major safety feature is that there is no huge, hulking pitcher. Instead, the batter swings at a ball resting on top of a tee. This reduces the risk of injury. Not to mention walks, strike outs, wild pitches, balks, arguments with the umpire and players racing from the dugouts to fight with the pitcher.

I find a spot on the sidelines just as the first batter steps up to the tee. He is wearing a batting helmet on top of his baseball cap.

"Why is he wearing a batting helmet?" I ask the parent next to me. "There's no pitcher."

"I don't know. I think it's in case they hit themselves in the back of the head with the bat."

"That's ridiculous."

The first batter swings. He misses the ball and hits himself in the back of the head with the bat. It turns out to be one of the better hits of the evening. His second swing sends the ball dribbling back to the second baseman. Alert fielding holds it to a triple. There goes the tee's no-hitter.

By the time my kid gets up to bat, there have been seven errors, one triple and a pair of inside-the-infield home runs. As my kid picks up a bat, a lady approaches me.

"Is that your child?" she asks.

"Yes, why?"

"Good. Then you'll want to sign this."

"I've already signed up for the team photo."

"This is for post-game drinks."

"That sounds great. I'm sure I'll need one."

"For the children. Each week a parent is supposed to bring drinks for the entire team."

I sign the sheet saying that I will be happy to provide soft drinks for my kid's entire team so that each of them can have more sugar in their systems and bigger and better cavities. By the time I finish, my kid is standing on third base.

"How did he get there?" I ask the parent next to me.

"He skipped second."

An hour later, the game ends. I head toward the car with my kid. I am nearly there when another woman approaches me. She is holding a sign-up sheet in her hand.

"Now what?"

"Car pool list," she says. "Sign here."

I sign a sheet saying that I will be thrilled to death to pick up a carload of kids each week so that on the way home they will have some place to spill the soft drinks I have bought for them.

A wonderful thing, T-ball. Gives parents something to do to keep them out of trouble.

The following year, the six-year-old advances to Little League. I drive him to the first practice.

Due to scheduling problems, his team will not be able to use the well-groomed field for their first few practices. Luckily, the coach owns a farm, with plenty of room behind the barn.

When we arrive at the coach's farm, a dozen kids in various shapes and sizes already are there playing catch. Some are skilled, but most have trouble keeping their caps on and catching the ball at the same time. It looks like a scene out of *Bad News Bears*. Or a Cleveland Indians' game.

I walk him to the field behind the barn. Cows are mooing in an adjacent field. A large pig is rooting in a nearby pen. I stand along the sidelines, upwind from the pen, and watch the practice.

After several minutes of practice, the coach walks over to where I am standing. I introduce myself.

"I imagine this is the first time you've had a boy in Little League," he says.

"Well, yes," I admit. "How did you know?"

"Parents who have had kids in Little League for a while usually don't hang around practices much."

"You mean most of the parents don't stand on the sidelines and encourage their children to do their very best?"

"Most of the parents cruise past the field at about 40 miles an hour and tell the kid to jump out."

"I don't understand."

"You will if you stick around."

After a few minutes of loosening up, the coach calls for batting practice. He tells one kid to bat and the rest to take the field.

"I'll do the pitching," he says, walking to a makeshift mound. "Oh, and we'll need an adult to handle the catching. None of the kids are ready to do that yet."

I look around me. The only ones left on the sideline are me and the pig. And the pig looks like a third baseman.

I pick up a spare glove and crouch down behind the plate. A seven-year-old digs into the batter's box. The coach grooves a practice pitch right down the middle. The kid swings and misses the ball by a mile. I miss the ball by two miles.

"Sorry," I call to the coach as I scramble back to retrieve the ball. "I'm a little rusty."

I pick up the ball and fire it back. It sails four feet over the coach's glove. The second baseman runs over to pick it up and toss it back to the mound.

"Sorry," I call to the second baseman.

The coach grooves another one. The batter misses another one. I miss another one. I retrieve the ball and throw it back.

"Sorry," I call to the second baseman.

Ten pitches later, the batter has no hits, I have no catches and the second baseman is calling for oxygen.

Another batter steps in. He drills the first pitch. Straight back. I have no time to react before the ball hits me in the shoulder.

"That's the way to get your body in front of the ball," the coach calls.

"It was nothing."

On the next nine pitches, the kid hits seven foul balls, four of which hit me in the shins, two of which hit me in the chest and one of which temporarily renders me a soprano.

By the time practice is over, I am barely able to walk off the field. As I head for the sidelines, the coach thanks me for helping out and invites me to come back for the next practice.

I think I know why. If I don't show up, he's going to have to buy a chest protector for the pig.

Fortunately, our 12-year-old shows no interest in playing Little League. Unfortunately, he decides to join a swim team.

There are few sports events that last as long as swim meets. In fact, there are few sports seasons that last as long as swim meets.

When parents go to Little League games or soccer matches, a lot of them bring along something to read. Like a newspaper or a magazine. When parents go to their kids' swim meets, they bring along *War and Peace*.

None of which concerns me much until the 12-year-old freestyles his way onto the team at our swimming club. It comes to my attention that the 12-year-old has freestyled his way onto the team when I walk into the living room on a Saturday afternoon and find him sprawled inertly on the couch.

"Why are you lying on the couch?" I ask. "On Saturdays you're supposed to be mowing the lawn."

"I can't, Dad," he sighs between barely moving lips. "Coach said we should always rest up before a meet."

"Oh, of course. What time is the meet?"

"Next Thursday at 7:30."

On Thursday we wade through knee-high grass to the garage, get into the car and drive to where the swim meet is to be held. Although we never have been to this particular pool before, we have no trouble finding it. We just follow the smell of the brownies.

They always have brownies at swim meets. That's because the parents of the swimmers on the host team bring them to the meet and sell them to help defray expenses. I'm not exactly sure what kind of expenses are involved in running a swim meet. It's not as if they're laying out big bucks for uniforms.

In any event, we park the car and walk to the pool, past a parents' booth containing enough brownies, cookies and cupcakes to rot every tooth east of the Mississippi. As the sun begins its gentle slide in the western sky, we find a couple of spots at the edge of the pool, open our lawn chairs and sit down to watch the warmups.

There are three teams in the meet, and they take turns hopping into the pool to get acclimated. Every kid who hops in has tan skin, long arms and a flat belly. I remember when I had a flat belly. Of course, I remember when cars had running boards.

After half an hour of warmups it is time for the meet to begin. The first event is the 42-foot freestyle race for kids six and under. Forty-two feet might not seem like much of a distance, but it is when you're only 41 inches tall.

Four girls who are six and under climb up onto the starting blocks. Five judges watch intently as the gun goes off. Ten people with stop watches hanging around their necks walk over and stand in front of where we are sitting. For the next 30 seconds we hear a great deal of yelling and splashing. It sounds like a terrific race.

Before the next event begins, we get up and move our lawn chairs to a new location. The meet continues. We see 7- and 8-year-olds swim relays. We see 9- and 10-year-olds swim backstrokes. What we do not see is our 12-year-old anywhere near the water.

Finally, as the moon hangs silver in the sky, it is his turn. He climbs onto the starting block, the gun goes off and he swims freestyle for 50 meters. He does not win, but he makes a respectable showing for his first meet of the season.

"That was great," I tell him as he walks over to where we are sitting and drips chlorine on my slacks. "Better hurry up now and get your stuff so we can leave. It's getting late."

"Dad, I can't leave yet," he says. "I'm in another event."

"Another event. We've already been here most of the summer. How can they possibly have any more events left?"

"Well, they do. There are 61 events altogether."

"Terrific. Which one are you in next?"

"Number 60."

As the moon hovers golden in the sky, we wait for his next

event, the freestyle relay for 11- and 12- year-olds. The more we wait, the more certain I am that he will do well in the race. But why shouldn't he? By the time they get to the 11 - 12 freestyle relay, he'll be 16.

At last it is time for his relay, which he and his teammates win handily. We fold up our lawn chairs and head for the car. Ahead of us, I see a faint glow of light just above ground level. It's probably the headlights of the other cars pulling out of the parking lot.

On the other hand, it could be the sun rising.

But there is one sport that doesn't cost much, doesn't hurt much and never seems to last too long.

We call it basement basketball.

I suppose if my old man had been able to hug me once in a while, basement basketball might never have been invented. But my old man was not the hugging type. He was my old man. Not my father, not my pop, not my daddy. He was my old man, and when he came home from work there was grease under his fingernails and metal chips in his hair and his work clothes smelled of oil.

He would shower and change and eat dinner, and then he would sit in his chair and read his paper, just like Archie Bunker. And he never, ever hugged me.

It just wasn't his style. I suspect that his old man never hugged him and that I come from a long line of old men who did not hug each other. On the day I graduated from college, he held out his hand and I shook it, and I still can remember the way it felt. I think that was the last time my old man and I ever touched.

When I became an old man, hugging my first child was easy. But that's because she was a girl. Fathers always have been allowed to hug their daughters. It's practically a requirement for the job.

Even when our first boy was born, there was a certain amount of hugging for a while.

There was a hug when I went off to work, a hug and a kiss on those nights I was home for his bedtime. Sometimes he would sit quietly on my lap and we would read a book or watch television or just talk, and I would sort of casually rest my hand on his arm or on his leg and feel the magical blend of softness and strength that is a growing child.

But then he grew too much.

He was eight, maybe nine, when the kisses stopped. And, soon after, there were no more hugs. He was too big for that stuff. Too old. There still were hugs and kisses for his mother. There is, I am sure, a lifetime supply for her.

But, for his old man, he had reached the age of, "Well, good night, Dad."

I wanted to stop him the first time he said that. I wanted to pull him back and put my arms around his shoulders and hold him with all the love that was in me and whisper in his ear that he would never, ever, be too big for his old man to hug him.

But I didn't. I couldn't. I didn't know how.

So I invented basement basketball.

It's a silly game, really, a game for which the rules are not very well defined or the equipment necessarily suitable.

It is played with a pink beachball and a clothes basket perched on a bench in the basement. Sometimes the clothes basket has to be emptied before we can use it, and frequently the game is interrupted by a shout from the laundry room demanding to know why her clean clothes are sitting in a pile on top of the dryer. Basement basketball is not her favorite game.

Four of us play it. The 12-year-old is on my team. His little brothers are on the other team. To make it more fair, our team plays on its knees. The object is to get the ball into the clothes basket.

But that's not really the object. Because, as we play it, the game is sort of like basketball and sort of like hockey and a great deal like big-time wrestling. Sometimes there are spectacular shots and sometimes pictures get knocked off of walls, and every once in a while a little boy lands on the floor a little too hard, and there is time out for tears.

Mostly, however, there is a lot of grabbing and holding and illegal hugging. And at least once every game, four bodies wind up in one large giggling pile in the middle of the basement carpet. And frequently a voice from upstairs in the kitchen warns us to take it easy before someone gets hurt or something gets broken.

But I'm not worried about those things. I'm only worried that someday, long before I am ready for it to happen, my sons will grow too big for basement basketball.

13
Claws

When we decided to get married, it was with the understanding that no cats would ever enter our vine-covered cottage.

"I don't like cats," I explained to the woman who had agreed to love, honor and stop my howling. "Cats are disloyal."

And she murmured: "Yes, dear."

"Not only that, they are sneaky."

"Yes, dear."

"And arrogant."

"Yes, dear."

At last the big day arrived and we walked down the aisle. We exchanged our rings and our vows and then the minister pronounced us man and wife. I turned to her, lifted her veil, looked into the lovely face of my blushing new bride.

And she murmured: "Not even a cute little Siamese?"

But I stuck to my guns and we were well into our second week of wedded bliss before we got a cat. His name was Charlie and he was a stray who wandered in one night to share our $40-a-month apartment, our meager possessions and our leftover macaroni and cheese. After two weeks of leftover macaroni and cheese, Charlie took a hike. Cats may be disloyal, sneaky and arrogant, but they are not stupid.

Whatever else it did, I think maybe the episode taught her a lesson. After that, there was no more talk of cats.

Of course, part of the reason for that may have been that a short time later the population explosion began to leave its fallout all over our house. With four kids and a dog, the last thing we needed was another warm body standing in front of the refrigerator.

It is with considerable surprise, therefore, that I arrive home from work one day in the middle of the week to see a small, white kitten lying on our living room floor.

He is maybe eight weeks old, with dark markings on the top of his head and a raccoon-striped tail. And a right leg that bends unnaturally beneath him as he lies there, sleeping fiercely.

She was driving home from the store, she explains, when she heard crying coming from behind a bush on the side of the road. So she got out, in the rain, poked around in the wet and mud of the vacant lot and found him lying there, soaking, scrawny, obviously in pain.

She drove him to the vet, where the diagnosis was a probable broken leg, a possible broken pelvis. The vet can fix it for $100. Or end it for $10. Instead she brought him home, cleaned him up, coaxed him into eating a tiny little bit of food borrowed from a neighbor. And now he is sleeping on the floor in the middle of my living room and I don't like cats any more than I ever did. Especially one that would cost me $100.

"He must have been hit by a car," she says, "and somebody just drove away and left him there. Isn't that awful?"

"It certainly is," I agree. I am, after all, not entirely devoid of the milk of human kindness. "When are you getting rid of him?"

"Well, the animal shelter is closed for the day. But I'll telephone them tomorrow morning."

"Don't forget," I say, reaching out to touch the helpless little creature that will be spending this one night with us. You can still see the scars on the inside of my right wrist.

"Even though he's only going to be here overnight, we ought to have a name for him," she says.

"How about Midnight?" I suggest.

"That's a pretty common name for a cat," she points out.

"Not for a white one," I point out.

"I don't like it," she says. "I think we should call him Fairfield. That's the name of the road where I found him."

"That's a terrible name. How about Rover?"

The discussion ends, as most of our discussions do, with no decision.

That evening, the kitten with no name begins to stir, straining to get to his feet, failing, settling instead for dragging himself along the rug on his belly to explore his new surroundings. She feeds him some more food, fills a jigsaw puzzle box with borrowed cat litter, lifts him into it . . . and out again when he is finished.

As the evening goes on, the kitten seems to take on strength. On three legs he stands, begins to walk, falls but gets up again. Reaching the sofa, he climbs, his front claws stretching, but his back leg unable to support him.

He falls on his side, gets up, tries again—a game, pathetic attempt, destined to fail. He is one tough little kitty. It is hard not to be impressed by his courage.

At bedtime she finds a blue basket, lines it with a towel and lifts him into it. The basket goes on the floor beside our bed, where she can reach it in the middle of the night if necessary.

When I awaken in the morning, the first thing I see is him dragging himself gamely across the floor—his right back leg trailing limp and useless behind him—to play with my slipper.

As I leave for work, I remind her not to forget to call the animal shelter.

"You know I don't like cats," I say as I walk out to my car.

For reasons not entirely clear to me, the phone call to the animal shelter misses connections and when I come home for dinner the kitten is still there. In my recliner.

"They're supposed to call back first thing tomorrow," she says.

"They'd better. You know I don't like cats," I say, taking a seat on the floor next to my recliner.

In the morning, the phone rings. She answers it.

"It's the woman from the . . . from that place," she says, covering the mouthpiece with her hand. "What should I tell her?"

I look at the kitten curled up in the blue basket beside our bed, white paws covering his nose, right leg bent unnaturally underneath him.

"Tell her . . . tell her to forget it."

For the first few months that he lives with us, Fairfield is content to sit around the house, looking cute, rubbing his furry little white body against my dark green suit and making one corner of the basement smell very, very bad.

Then the warm weather comes and he takes his act outside. He begins sitting in the front yard, looking cute, rubbing his furry little body against the mailman's dark gray suit and making the sandbox in the neighbor's yard smell very, very bad.

And he begins to hunt, his injured leg growing stronger with each expedition.

He catches little things at first. Grasshoppers. June bugs. Badminton birds. But then, one evening as I am standing on the front porch, he trots around the corner of the house from the backyard, making a high, squealing sound.

I move closer to investigate The high, squealing sound, it turns out, is not being made by the cat. It is being made by the bunny he is holding in his mouth. Either that or the cat has taught himself ventriloquism.

I am surprised. I didn't know rabbits could make noise. I thought they just stood around wriggling their noses, eating carrots and being fruitful.

"Drop that bunny," I shout at the cat. The cat ignores me. I run toward him. He runs away, still holding the bunny in his mouth. I chase him. Around the yard, up the driveway, into the garage, yelling "drop that bunny" at the top of my lungs. Across the street, my neighbor steps out on his front porch to see what I am doing. He sees me running around in my garage yelling "drop that bunny." He steps back inside his house. He locks his door.

Eventually the cat tires of the game and drops the bunny. It hops away. It doesn't seem to be seriously hurt, but it is obvious that it is plenty irritated.

Later that night I am discussing the incident with the woman who promised to love, honor and bring out the beast in me.

"I don't think he was really going to eat that rabbit," she says. "I think he was just satisfying his basic instincts as a hunter and he was bringing his catch home to show us."

"On the other hand, maybe it was his way of telling us he's getting tired of macaroni and cheese."

"Well, I think we'd better do something about it," she says.

"What do you suggest?"

"We'll have him de-clawed. And, as long as we have him in there, we might as well get him neutered, too."

I agree, even though it sounds sort of severe just for catching one little rabbit.

It costs us $100 to have the cat altered to our specifications. Three days later I get a call at work.

"What do you think is on the floor of our garage?" a familiar voice demands.

"A puddle of oil?"

"No. It's a mouse. A dead mouse. And how do you think he died?"

"Maybe it was a heart attack. Was he wearing a jogging suit?"

"Very funny. It was the cat who killed him."

"So why are you calling me at work?"

"I just thought you should know."

I thank her for interrupting me in the middle of my work day to tell me that there is a dead mouse on the floor of our garage and I hang up.

Even without claws, we discover, our cat is probably the most efficient killing machine this side of Bruce Lee. I'm not sure who this cat's father was, but I wouldn't be surprised if he was the mascot for Murder, Inc. In the next month there is not a bird, mouse or rabbit in the neighborhood that does not suffer a loss in the family.

The topper comes when we arrive home from a dining engagement to find something gray and lifeless lying in the middle of the family room rug.

"Oh my God," she screams, dropping her Burger Chef cup, "it's a big mouse."

"Or a small kangaroo."

"Is it dead?" she demands.

"How should I know?" I say.

"Well why don't you get down off that chair and find out?"

The mouse is, indeed, exceptionally dead. Another victim of our killer cat.

"That does it," she says, reaching for the phone.

"Don't turn him in," I plead. "Give him another chance. He comes from a broken home. It was only temporary insanity. Let him try shock probation. I know he'll never do it again if only . . ."

"Don't be ridiculous," she says. "I'm not calling the cops. I'm calling the pet store to order one of those collars with bells on it."

After that our cat wears a collar with little bells on it, and when he tries to sneak up on his prey the little bells warn them before he can get close enough to pounce. Which is terrific for all the small animals in our neighborhood but very frustrating for the cat, who spends more and more of his time moping around the house.

Not that I blame him.

When you've been belled, de-clawed and neutered, what sense does it make to go out?

Even though he can no longer do Al Capone imitations, Fairfield can be a real pain. From three rooms away he learns to distinguish the sound of a can of tuna from a can of vegetable soup as it turns on the electric can opener. No box is too high for him to kick litter out of. In the evenings he learns to stand at the kitchen door and yowl for it to be opened. Which may or may not mean that he wants to go out. Sometimes it just means that he has an urge to watch somebody open a door.

He is an annoying little creature. But there are times when we have a schizo cat on our hands, a real Jekyll and Hyde.

Because this is the same cat who greets me with love in the morning, who springs up onto the kitchen counter and arches his back and narrows his eyes and insists that I pick him up. And clings to my shoulder as I pour my orange juice and brew my tea. And sits with me in my chair, the rumblings of his soft, small body warm and deep against my chest in the morning.

Because this is the same cat who curls up in the rocking chair in the evenings, a breathing Norman Rockwell painting that each time reminds me that the only thing as sensuously innocent as a sleeping child is a sleeping cat.

And late in the summer, a year after he arrives, the woman who promised to love, honor and tickle my chin discovers that she has an allergy. To cat hair.

"What does that mean?" I ask. "We have to get rid of him?"

"Either that or you have to shave him every morning."

It is not an easy thing, giving away a cat. But that is when you discover who your friends are.

Eventually, though, we hear of someone who might be interested. And she comes to our house, an attractive young woman who lives in an apartment and likes cats. And she takes him, the helpless, pathetic little creature that came to our house for the night and stayed for a year and left his white hair on our furniture and brought his victims to our doorstep and greeted me each morning with his arched back and his narrowed eyes and his warm, gentle purring.

"Think you'll miss him just a little?" asks the woman who promised to love, honor and tickle my chin as the young woman drives away with our cat.

"Who, me? Don't be silly. You know I don't like cats."

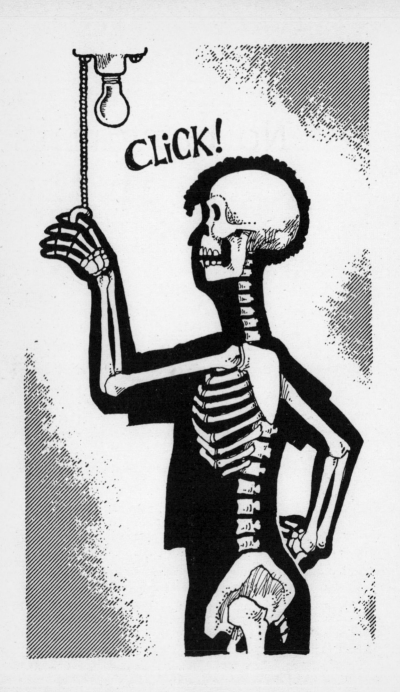

CLiCK!

14

No bargains in the basement

Even without a cat, it soon becomes obvious that our vine-covered cottage once again is becoming overcrowded.

We have a teenage girl who needs a bedroom, two phones and three bathrooms. All at the same time. We have a 12-year-old boy who can hit 23 consecutive foul shots but hasn't managed to swish a dirty sock into the clothes hamper in two years. We have a seven-year-old boy who owns the world's largest collection of Hot Wheels and parks them in the shag rug of the family room. We have a five-year-old boy who eats so much peanut butter that he sticks to the kitchen floor. We have a fat dog who gets a nervous tic if you ask her to get off the couch.

"Do you ever get the feeling that we should have built this house in the shape of a shoe?" I ask the woman who promised to love, honor and whip them all soundly and send them to bed.

"You're right," she says. "Maybe we should buy a bigger house."

"A bigger house? It's been five years since the last time we were able to afford the mortgage payments on this one. Besides, what I was thinking is that maybe I should fix up the basement. We could use part of it for a rec room and the other part could be an office for me."

"Well, maybe," she agrees. "But first you're going to have to do something about the moisture down there. It's terrible."

"Oh, you're exaggerating."

"How would you know? The only time you're ever down there is to pick mushrooms. And if you think I'm exaggerating, check out the north end of the basement."

"The north end? How the heck am I supposed to tell which is the north end?"

"Simple," she says, "just check which side of the water softener the moss is growing on."

The next day I visit a hardware store.

"I need a dehumidifier," I tell the man there.

"Fifteen, 20 or 30?" he asks.

"No, I think one will be enough."

"You don't understand," he says. "Dehumidifiers come in different sizes—15 pints, 20 pints or 30 pints."

"Well, I probably should get the biggest one and make sure I get all the moisture out of the air. How much does the 30-pint cost?"

"$250."

"Then again, if we take every little bit of moisture out of the air, our skin might dry out. How much is the 20-pint?"

"$230."

"In fact, it seems to me I remember reading somewhere that a good ratio of water to air is crucial in preventing cactus from growing in the cracks of your basement floor. How much is the 15-pint?"

"$210."

I thank the get-rich-quick hardware store man and head for a discount store.

Normally I avoid discount stores. I do this partly because I am allergic to fat ladies in pink hair curlers. But mostly I do it because discount stores tend to hire clerks who are on their break, on their lunch hour, on their way home, don't work in this department, don't know, don't remember, don't speak English or just plain don't give a damn.

But at the prices they're charging for dehumidifiers in hardware stores, I'll make an exception.

At the discount store I head directly for the ladies' shoe department, where I approach a clerk.

"Excuse me, I'm looking for a . . ."

"I don't work in this department."

"What department do you work in?"

"Hardware."

"Gotcha. I'm looking for a dehumidifier."

"You're looking for a dehumidifier in the ladies' shoe department?

"Of course not. But I knew if I asked a clerk in the hardware department he wouldn't work there. So I figured if I came right to the ladies' shoe department that I'd probably find . . ."

"Can you hurry this up, mister? I wanna go on my break before lunch hour."

"OK, so help me find a dehumidifier."

"They're in the jewelry department."

"The jewelry department? That's ridiculous. Who would want to wear a dehumidifier around their neck?"

"I don't know. And I don't give a damn. But they're there. Right next to small appliances."

"Which way to the jewelry department?"

"You see where that fat lady is standing," he says. "The one with the pink curlers in her hair?"

"Do you mean the one in the bright slacks and tennis shoes, or the one in the hot pants and high heels?"

"No, no. The one wearing the shower clogs and the 'I Love Conway Twitty' T-shirt."

"Oh. Right."

"OK. Go just past her and hang a left. The jewelry department is right there. You can't miss it. It's just the other side of the $2.99 original oil paintings."

I walk past the nattily attired lady until I reach the jewelry department, which is where I discover that I was right in the first place. It is ridiculous to say that they carry dehumidifiers in the jewelry department. In the jewelry department they carry typewriters, cameras, telescopes, stereos, Robert Conrad posters and humidifiers. Dehumidifiers are not carried anywhere in the store.

It takes three more stores, 12 more clerks on their lunch hours and 47 more fat ladies in pink hair curlers, but eventually I am able to locate a dehumidifier for $170 and soon it is sucking water out of my basement at the rate of 20 pints a day.

While the dehumidifier does its best to make the basement dry and the electric company rich, I start remodeling. I fasten studs to the walls. I nail paneling to the studs. I put in acoustical ceiling tiles. After a summer of chalk lines, plumb bobs, footers, headers and other words builders have invented to keep me confused, everything is finished but the lights and the carpet.

I ask my good neighbor Bill if he can recommend an electrician to install the lights.

"Electrician?" he says, "Why would you want to spend a lot of money on some expensive electrician? We can do the job ourselves."

"Do you really think so?"

"Of course. How hard can it be for two reasonably intelligent and skilled adults to hang a lamp?" he says, as we push a 2-by-4 into place to brace the patio cover we installed last summer.

"I don't know," I say.

"Believe me, there's nothing to it. Look, I've got this book at home that explains all about wiring and electricity."

While he goes to look for the book, I go into the house and mention to the woman who promised to love, honor and keep me grounded that we are going to install the lighting in the basement.

"After all, how hard can it be for two reasonably intelligent and skilled adults to hang a lamp?" I point out.

"Reasonably intelligent and skilled adults?" she says. "Oh, thank God. For a minute I was afraid you two dummies were going to do it yourselves."

The next morning my good neighbor Bill comes over with his book, *Up Your Amp*. We skim through it and then we drive to our neighborhood He-Man Hardware Store, the one where all the customers have steel rules on their belts and purple thumbnails on their hands. We purchase a two-bulb ceiling fixture, a pair of 40-inch fluorescent bulbs, some gray wire and assorted items known in technical circles as "electrical stuff."

We bring it all home and take it to the basement, where we open the box containing the two-bulb ceiling fixture. Like 10-speed bikes and every Christmas tree we've bought in the past five years, two-bulb ceiling fixtures come unassembled.

But with the skillful use of the proper tools, we assemble the two-bulb ceiling fixture in just three hours. When we are finished, we put away the pipe wrench and the tire iron and prepare to do the wiring.

To start, we remove the old fixture with a screwdriver. Which, it turns out, is not the best possible way we could have started. I realize that this is not the best possible way we could have started shortly after I hear the loud crackling noise and see the bright flash of light.

"Did we do something wrong?" I ask my good neighbor Bill, who is standing in the middle of my basement with a melted screwdriver in his hand and a funny look on his face.

"Uh, would you happen to know where your fuse box is?" asks my good neighbor Bill.

We locate the fuse box and we turn off the basement power. Connecting wires is a great deal easier when the power is off, we discover. In a matter of minutes my good neighbor Bill has the wires together.

"Turn on the power," he says.

I turn on the power. Turning on the power is followed by the flickering of the fluorescent light fixture coming to life. Which is followed by the voice of the woman who promised to love, honor and turn me on coming through the laundry chute.

"What the heck's going on down there?" she yells.

"Why?" I yell back.

"The light in the bathroom just went off."

"Probably a burned-out bulb."

"The lights also went off in the kitchen, the family room, the living room and the inside of the television set."

"Probably an incredible coincidence."

But, just to make her happy, we turn off the power in the basement, disconnect the wires in the fluorescent light, reverse them and re-connect them. This time when I turn on the power, the fluorescent light flickers on, but no voice comes down through the laundry chute.

My good neighbor Bill was right. There was nothing to it. In no time at all I have a fluorescent light glowing in my basement and as soon as it is carpeted and furnished it will be ready for a party.

Unfortunately, my good neighbor Bill won't be able to come, because he has moved away. He says he couldn't stand living next door to a fire hazard.

In my optimism (which is boundless) and my ignorance (which is colossal) I assumed that when my good neighbor Bill and I got the light fixture put up, the tough part of finishing off the basement was over. All that remained, I was sure, was to walk into a carpet store, tell the salesman what I wanted, give him my money and then sit back with a glass of chilled white wine while two workmen came out the next day and installed it.

Which is not the way it works.

First off, the woman who promised to love, honor and sweep my sawdust wants to know what color I plan to buy.

"I thought a nice pale yellow shag would be good," I say.

"Are you crazy?" she inquires. "Why would you buy a yellow rug?"

"Well, it would be a great place to housebreak the puppy."

"We don't have a puppy," she points out. "What we do have is four kids with big flat feet who would walk 20 miles out of their way to find a clump of dirt to track into the house."

"You're right. I'll buy a black carpet."

"That's just as bad. It doesn't show dirt, but you'll be able to see every speck of lint from here to the laundromat."

Eventually we agree upon a color and I go out to find a store that sells dirt-colored carpeting with white specks in it.

At the fourth store I visit, a salesman shows me exactly the carpet for which I am looking, priced at $8.98 a square yard, installed. I tell him the measurements of my basement, he whips out a pocket calculator and announces that the carpet will cost me $328.

"Terrific," I say. "I'll take it."

"Of course," he says, "you realize that at this price you're getting padding with it that may not stand up to hard traffic as well as more expensive padding. Do you plan to put this carpet where it will be getting heavy wear?"

"Define heavy wear."

"Will it be walked on by anyone who weighs more than 25 pounds?"

I decide to order the heavier padding, which costs $2 more per square yard, running the cost to $460, installed.

"When will it be delivered?" I ask.

"Well, first I have to come out and measure the area," he says.

"Measure the area? What for? I already told you the measurements."

"Yes, I know. But we've found that sometimes customers don't measure exactly right and then the carpet they order is not really the right size. To keep that from happening, I come out myself and measure it personally. Now, I can be there at 1 p.m. on Thursday or 3:30 on Friday. When will you be home?"

"I won't be home either time. I have to be at work. Isn't there some other time you could come out?"

"Certainly," he says, consulting his calendar. "What are you doing next Feb. 24th?"

The following Thursday, at 1 p.m., I take the afternoon off to meet the salesman and his ruler in my basement. His measurements, it turns out, are somewhat different from my measurements. $260 different. This brings the cost of the carpet to $720, installed.

"Let me explain our credit plans to you," he says after I have agreed to this most recent price. "We have our revolving charge, we have our 90 days same as . . ."

"I'll be paying cash."

"Please?"

"I said, I'll be paying cash."

"You're kidding. You mean you don't earn enough to qualify for Master Charge?"

"You don't understand. I don't like to charge things. So I saved my money until I had enough to pay for the carpet in cash. You do accept cash, don't you?"

"Well, sure, I suppose so. But I'm not sure exactly how to write this order up now. It's probably going to cause me a lot of extra paperwork."

"So how soon will you have my carpet installed?" I ask the salesman after I have talked him into accepting cash.

"Shouldn't be more than three weeks."

"Three weeks? Why does it take you so long?"

"We don't actually do the installation," he explains. "Another company takes care of that."

Four weeks later my basement floor is still as naked as the day it was born. I decided to call the carpet store.

"When is my carpet coming in?" I ask.

"Oh, it's been in for about two weeks," a voice on the phone says. "Did you want us to bring it out and install it?"

I pause to let that question sink in while I consider a number of responses:

(1) No, I wanted you to keep the carpet for which I paid $720 a month ago and every once in a while I planned to come to your store and look at it.

(2) Actually, I don't need a carpet. I just gave the salesman $720 because I was afraid that if I left it in the bank, inflation would eat it up.

(3) Yes, I would like to have it delivered, but not for several years because gray cement floors are still very trendy in our neighborhood.

Instead, I ask the voice on the phone if he would mind having the carpet brought to my house at his earliest convenience. Assuming, of course, this would not disrupt the normal operation of the store's business.

Two weeks later, the carpet finally is installed. Now the basement is perfect. It has a carpeted floor, paneled walls, lighted ceiling and dry air.

And nobody in the family will go down there. They all say it's too empty down there.

Which really doesn't bother me all that much, because it leaves plenty of room for a pool table.

All my life I have wanted to own a pool table. I guess it's because I formed my ideas of what was classy by watching old Cary Grant movies. And it seemed like old Cary was forever standing around in the billiard room of his heavily draped, 40-room mansion, swirling brandy in a snifter and saying really witty things to long-legged blondes.

So I married a long-legged blonde and saved my money. After five years I had enough cash to pay for a brandy snifter. But it takes 15 years to come up with enough to buy a pool table.

The news that I am about to sink my life savings into a pool table is greeted with some disfavor by the woman who promised to love, honor and keep me behind the eight ball. Fortunately, her aim is lousy and the brandy snifter shatters harmlessly on the wall behind me.

"You must have hit senility 30 years ahead of schedule," she snaps. "How can you think of putting all that money into something as useless as a pool table?"

"This is important to me," I explain. "All my life I've looked forward to having a pool table, so I could stand around it like Cary Grant, saying really witty things to long-legged blondes."

"So, even if you buy this stupid pool table, where are you going to find somebody to write really witty things for you to say?" she snickers.

"The same place I find someone who is really blonde to say them to," I retort. It is one of my all-time great comebacks, and it keeps me chuckling to myself all night long. On the couch.

The next day I go shopping for a pool table.

My first stop is at Benny's Bargain Billiards Barn. Benny himself meets me at the door. I can tell it's Benny, because his name is sewn in script over the pocket of his bowling shirt.

"C'mon in, friend," Benny says.

Immediately I am on my guard. Any salesman who calls you "friend" can be presumed to be 60 percent behind on his monthly quota and willing to take out a second mortgage on his mother's soul to get his hand in your wallet.

"What can we do for you today, friend?"

"Well, I'm looking for a pool table," I admit.

"Got just the thing for you," he says. "Right down here. Lemme clear my lunch off of it so you can get a real good look. It's a beauty, isn't it? I can have this little baby in your rumpus room by 5 o'clock today for just $299. You can't beat that price with a stick. Matter of fact, friend, if you come in here tomorrow that price tag's gonna say $1,499."

"It does sound like a pretty good price," I agree, looking over the table. "I can't help but notice, though, that this table only has four pockets. I was sort of hoping to find one that had all six."

"Oh, you want the deluxe model? Why didn't you say so in the first place. Follow me. We've got a terrific deal waitin' for you, good buddy, with a pocket at every corner and one at each side for no extra charge. I can let you have it for $599."

"It does look a bit nicer. Does it have a slate bed?"

"Come again?"

"A slate bed. I understand the very best pool tables are made with one-inch-thick Italian slate beds."

"Don't you believe it, pal. That's just a story made up by them Eye-talians to put real American pool table manufacturers out of business. The truth is, the very best tables are made right here in this country with real American manmade materials."

"What exactly is the bed of this table made from, then?"

"Drywall."

I thank Benny, edge out of the store and head for a place that sells higher quality pool tables. A salesman meets me at the door.

"I'd like to look at your pool tables," I tell him.

"Did you have an appointment, sir?" he asks.

"Gosh, I didn't know I needed one."

The salesman looks me up and down as if I have just torn a six-inch gash in the felt.

"Well, perhaps we could slip you in without one," he says. "Our 2 p.m. client was forced to postpone. Something about trouble with the Bentley."

He guides me into the showroom.

"This is a very nice model," he says, indicating a beautiful table. "It has a one-inch Italian slate bed, hand-rubbed mahogany rails, custom-crafted cushions, 24-carat gilt legs and Moroccan leather pockets."

"It's perfect . . ."

"The price is $6,000."

". . . then again, Moroccan leather probably would clash with our dinette set."

Eventually, we find a table that fits my budget. I tell the salesman it's for the servants.

A few days later the table is delivered by two men who carry it down to my basement and spend more than three hours setting it up. Then they are gone, and I am standing beside my pool table in my heavily mortgaged, seven-room aluminum-sided home. Casually, I swirl the Mountain Dew in my Tupperware glass.

I wonder if Cary has an extra-long-legged blonde he could lend me?

Not that I have all that much spare time to fritter away sinking nine balls in the corner pocket. Most of my evenings in the basement, it seems, are spent doing "little jobs."

Like fixing bicycles.

As I remember them, bikes had handlebars, a seat, a chain, two wheels and they ran forever. You could pedal a bike through World War II and nothing would go wrong with it.

Today, bikes have rat-trap pedals, derailleur gears, cotterless cranks, quick-release hubs, four-speed transmissions, radial tires, power disc brakes, AM-FM radios, and they last once around the block.

The last three bikes we bought fell apart under the Christmas tree. At any given moment there are enough bicycle parts in our basement to get Wilbur and Orville started all over again.

What makes it all so frustrating is that most of the bikes are sitting with their kickstands in the air because of minor problems. If a front wheel is missing, I know exactly what to do: take it to the repair shop. But the jobs that are too small for the repair shop are the ones that get me. One orange reflector coming loose on a rear fender can keep me up to my elbows in axle grease for a week. I once spent an entire summer trying to get a red rubber grip wriggled onto a handlebar.

The time the nut fell off is a perfect example.

I find out about it just as dinner is ending. The seven-year-old looks over a pile of never-to-be-eaten green beans and asks:

"Dad, can you fix my bike tonight?"

"What's wrong with it?"

"There's something wrong with the front wheel."

"Is it missing?" I ask, hopefully.

"No. Just some little part fell off and now the wheel rubs. Can you fix it?"

"I'll try."

"I'll get the bike," says the seven-year-old.

"I'll get the tool box," says the 12-year-old.

"I'll get the gin," says the woman who promised to love, honor and pour my doubles.

The seven-year-old and I carry the bike down to the basement, and I examine it. It is just as he said. A nut is missing from one side of the front axle. All I have to do is find a new one, tighten it on and the bike will be fixed.

I squat down and begin to rummage through the tool box for the right nut. The seven-year-old squats down beside me. There is a look of faithful confidence on his face.

After 10 minutes of sorting through rusty screws, bent nails, twisted shower curtain hooks, broken window shade brackets and smiling golf balls, I find a nut that is the right size.

"I'll have this thing fixed in a minute," I tell the seven-year-old. He nods. There is a look of patient understanding on his face.

I start to thread the nut onto the axle, using an adjustable wrench. After several dozen brisk turns, I release the adjustable wrench. The nut falls off and rolls under the washing machine.

"Why did you do that, Dad?" the seven-year-old asks. There is a look of puzzled concern on his face.

"The threads are stripped. The dummy who put this nut on originally got it on crosswise and really messed it up. Whoever did it must have been a real mechanical moron."

"You did it, Dad. Remember? You had to put it together for my birthday, and it took almost all day, and you broke your hammer and Mom yelled at you for saying . . ."

"Never mind. It's not important."

After an hour of twisting, I am convinced that the nut will not go on the axle. The only solution is to remove the axle from the wheel, put the nut on the other end, thread it all the way across and then put the wheel back on the bike.

I explain all of this to the seven-year-old. There is a look of stunned disbelief on his face.

I try to remove the wheel from the bike. I am not sure who put the nut on the other end of the axle, but I'm pretty sure it wasn't me. I think it was the Incredible Hulk. All the king's horses and all the king's blowtorches could not remove that nut.

After two hours of watching me wage war on his bike, the seven-year-old gives up and goes to bed. There is a look of surly disgust on his face.

Shortly before midnight, the wheel gives up and falls off the bike. Two spokes are broken. The axle is snapped. There are grease smears on my legs, face, arms and neck. My hands are as black as an editor's heart.

A week later the grease still is under my fingernails. The wheel still is on the floor of the basement. The seven-year-old has to run along behind his friends when they pedal off on their bikes to play. I feel sort of sorry for him.

On the other hand, he's the only kid in the neighborhood with four unicycles.

15

Don't just sit there smiling, DO something

Of course, when you have children, it is not enough to put a roof over their heads, food in their bellies, braces on their teeth, stereo headphones on their ears, $35 jeans on their bodies and combs in their back pockets.

You also have to DO things with them.

Sociologists, psychologists, educators and parents' organizations all agree that it is essential for the development of children that their fathers DO things with them. As far as I know, no one has ever asked an actual father. Or an actual child.

Unfortunately, the woman who promised to love, honor and read every article in *Parents Magazine* takes all of these theories very seriously.

"If you don't DO things with your children, they'll grow up to be maladjusted, antisocial cretins with vulgar, disgusting personal habits and a chronic inability to hold decent jobs."

"That's ridiculous," I counter. "My old man never DID things with me."

"I know."

"Well, okay. What kind of things am I supposed to DO with them?"

"Oh, I don't know. How about taking them roller skating? Remember how much fun that was when we were kids? Rolling along the sidewalk, with the wind blowing in our hair. The sensation of the wheels going clickity-click over the cracks. The sound of . . ."

"Spike stealing my Milk Duds."

"Huh?"

"Spike Nugent. Every time I tried to roller skate, Spike would steal my Milk Duds."

"I don't understand."

"Spike was the toughest kid on our block," I explain, "with a mean streak a mile wide. When I was five years old, I used to skate down the hill in front of my house. Spike would wait until I was going at top speed and then throw a tricycle in front of me. I'd hit the tricycle, fall down, tear my pants and skin my knees. And, while I was lying there, crying, Spike would run up and steal the Milk Duds out of my pocket."

"That's terrible. What a nasty child Spike must have been."

"Yeah. I often wondered what made her so mean."

"I can see why you weren't too thrilled about skating then," she says. "But how about later? How about when we were in fifth and sixth grade and we'd take our skates to school and play with them at recess? Remember that? Hurrying to the playground with our skate keys on strings around our necks. Tightening up the skates as hard as we could so they didn't slip off of our shoes. Racing around the outside of the basketball court. The feel of the blacktop under our skates. The sound of . . ."

"Spike stealing my Milk Duds."

"Again?"

"Yep. Spike hated me in fifth grade because I got more votes than she did when they had the class election."

"What were you running for?"

"Boys' restroom monitor. Anyway, she used to stand around at recess and wait for us to organize a relay race. Then, whenever my team was ahead, she'd wait until I came by and throw a bicycle out in front of me. And, while I was lying there, crying, my pants torn, my knees skinned up, she'd steal my Milk Duds."

"It must have been very traumatic for you."

"Not only that, it was painful. One time she knocked out two of my teeth."

"How awful."

"Not really. They probably would have fallen out from eating all those Milk Duds anyway."

"I'm sorry to hear about all your troubles with Spike. But I really wasn't planning on having us roller skate on the sidewalk or at a playground. I thought that we could go to a roller rink. Remember doing that in ninth grade?"

"Yeah."

"Gliding over the smooth wooden floor. The organ playing "Down by the Old Mill Stream." The sound of . . ."

"Spike stealing my Milk Duds."

"Oh for goodness sakes."

"Well, it's true. Every time I went to the Rollerdome, Spike would be there with her boyfriend, Frankie DeSpizio. They'd stand around smoking Luckies and rolling up their T-shirt sleeves and cracking their knuckles. And they'd wait for me to come rolling by real fast and then Spike would throw . . ."

"I know, I know. Spike would throw a motorcycle out in front of you."

"Naw. She'd throw Frankie DeSpizio. See, Frankie was about six inches shorter than she was and . . ."

"Oh, shut up and eat a Milk Dud while I go get the kids."

The news that the whole family is going roller skating is greeted with a certain amount of subtle skepticism by the 15-year-old.

Or, as she phrases it:

"Even YOU?"

"I'll have you know, young lady, that I was roller skating before you were born."

"Yeah. But now you're practically senile."

"So I'll wear orthopedic skates."

As we drive to the roller rink, it occurs to me that roller skating wasn't always a bad experience as a kid. Not every memory includes Spike Nugent. The good memories come flooding back:

Rolling effortlessly with the flow of other skaters at the roller rinks. Bending into the turns. Gliding into the straightaways. All the while, a man in the organ loft playing "Down by the Old Mill Stream," "Beautiful Ohio" and all the other lovely melodies so much a part of the activity. By the time we pull into the parking lot of the skating rink, I am humming "Skater's Waltz." Dah, dah, duh, dah.

We hurry through the parking lot. I open the door of the skating rink. A blast of noise hits me square in the ear. It is not music played by a man on an organ up in a loft. It is a record played by an adolescent on a stereo speaker system. Amplified to the threshold of pain. I do not instantly recognize the song that is causing my semicircular canals to flood over their banks, but I am pretty sure it is not "Down by the Old Mill Stream." As nearly as I can figure it, the name of the song is "C'mon, Mama, Shake Your Boogie."

We walk into the rink. Past the snack bar, which offers corn dogs, pizza, potato chips and all the other essentials of a good diet. Through the game room, where kids who have paid $2.25 to come in and skate are furiously engaged in not skating as they play pinball machines and football games.

The place is jammed with people, not a one of whom is old enough to remember when guitars could be played even during a power failure.

I walk up to the skate rental desk.

"I'll need size 10½," I tell the kid behind the desk.

"Skates don't come in half sizes," he says.

"But feet do," I point out.

"I don't make the rules, Pops," the kid says.

For a moment I consider telling the kid where he can roll his skates. But then I realize that gliding into the straightaways will not be half as much fun without skates. So I get a pair of size 10 and tell my toes to take turns breathing.

We take our rented skates and sit on a bench to put them on. The adolescent puts on a new record. The name of this one is "C'mon, Mama, Wiggle Your Boogie." By the time we finish lacing up our skates, the record is done. The adolescent says something into the microphone. It comes out over the amplified speaker system sounding something like, "Creek frammer fleegle gorp."

"What'd he say?" I ask, turning to the woman who promised to love, honor and carry me across the generation gap.

"Creek frammer fleegle gorp," she says.

The adolescent makes a bunch of other equally helpful announcements. When he gets to "Snarv, requith, nommer dube bifrit," there is a stampede of skaters out onto the track.

Cautiously, I join it.

My first few strides are halting and uncertain. I stick to the outside of the track, near the rail. It is slow going, but I work my way all the way around without falling. I decide to try another lap. With my eyes open.

Emboldened by yet another stand-up lap, I decide to move away from the rail and get into the flow of traffic. I drift over to my left. Skillfully I insert myself into the flow of traffic. Skillfully I watch the flow of traffic roar past me. Traffic flows a lot faster than I remembered it.

Blurs of denim streak past me on all sides. Teenage boys shove past me. Teenage girls cut in front of me. Little bitty kids duck under me. This isn't roller skating, it's demolition derby. The only consolation I can find in all of this is that while these kids are in here, skating, they aren't out on the highway, driving.

I decide to get out of the flow of traffic.

Which is when I discover the horrible truth: There are no exit ramps. Once you are in the flow of traffic, you stay in the flow of traffic. I am trapped. For 18 laps. While the amplified speakers blare "C'mon, Mama, Wiggle Your Shake."

Finally the song ends and the flow of traffic carries me off the track. Shaking and aching, I make my way to where the woman who promised to love, honor and fill my tub with Epsom Salts is sitting.

"I think I've had it," I wheeze. "Let's go home."

"Shnark gribble jakalg rawlik," she says.

I return the rental skates, round up our kids and leave the roller rink. Even if I was crazy enough to risk my life again in that teenaged Indy 500, I don't think I could take much more of that music.

I hate to admit that I don't like my kids' music. Because when I was growing up in the land of do-wop, do waddy waddy, do-wop, my old man never missed a chance to let me know what he thought of the music I favored.

"You call that music," he would scoff. "It sounds like a bunch of alley cats yowling. And why do you have to play it so loud? You're gonna drive us all crazy with that stuff."

I would suffer these diatribes in silence, because I had long ago given up trying to explain the aesthetic value of Bobby Freeman singing, "Do ya, do ya, do ya, do ya wanna dance" to a man who grew up with such lyrics as "Does eat oats and mares eat oats and little lambs eat ivy."

But inwardly I promised myself that when I had kids I would never make fun of their music and I would even sit and listen with them while they played their Little Richard records.

Eventually I left the land of do-wop, do waddy waddy, do-wop. I learned to twist and pony and frug. All night long. My hair grew longer, yeah, yeah, yeah. I plugged my ears into a system that used enough juice to light up Nova Scotia.

As I doddered into my 30s, I realized that I was losing touch. Not only did I no longer know where I was coming from, I wasn't quite sure why I had gone there. But I stuck to my vow of musical tolerance.

And then my 12-year-old discovers KISS.

I am made aware that my 12-year-old has discovered KISS on the day I hear sounds too horrible to describe coming from the basement. Screaming and yelling. Shouts of pain.

I run to the basement door.

"I don't know what you're doing to that dog," I yell down, "but stop it before she bites you."

"The dog's not even down here," yells back the 12-year-old. "That's my new KISS album."

"Well, then, you're playing it on the wrong speed. Try 33 ⅓."

"Very funny, Dad. You just don't appreciate modern music."

"Don't be silly. I love modern music."

"Yeah? Like who?"

"The Bee Gees and Rod Stewart and Barry Manifold and . . ."

"That's Manilow."

"Whatever."

"Anyway, Dad, those guys are old. They're practically back in the days of Elmer Presley."

"That's Elvis."

"Whatever."

"So what makes you think KISS is so great?" I ask.

With an animation noticeably lacking from his discussions of what's going on in school, he tells me more than I ever wanted to know about KISS.

Their names are Gene, Paul, Peter and Ace. In addition to spitting blood, breathing fire, belching smoke from their guitars and all those other musical standbys, the members of the group always wear makeup. No one, in fact, has ever seen them without makeup. It is suspected by some people that this is because they were born without faces.

The 12-year-old hands me a trading card.

"This will tell you all about them," he says.

The card has a picture of Gene on the front. He is all in chrome and black leather, with flame painting on his face. Seeing him, I am overwhelmed by a feeling of nostalgia for my '56 Chevy.

On the back of the card is biographical information:

"Gene, a notorious fire-breathing reptilian and bass guitarist extraordinaire, has established himself as one of the driving forces behind KISS' dynamic visual appeal. His bass guitar quivers the message of his fearsome power."

I am impressed. None of the music stars of my youth was a

fire-breathing reptilian. Most of them just drank beer and fooled around.

While I leaf through additional KISS material, the 12-year-old plays some more of their songs. "Gold Gin." "Hotter Than Hell." "Rock Bottom." And, of course, the lovely and melodic "Ladies Room."

But the more I listen, the more I am convinced that what I am really hearing are recordings of a bunch of alley cats yowling. And why does he have to play them so loud? He's gonna drive us all crazy with that stuff.

Sh-bop, sh-bop.

Not only are parents expected to tolerate their childrens' music, they are expected to take a vital interest in their school activities.

Even open houses.

When our first-born embarked upon the path of education, we were thrilled when it finally came time to go to her first open house.

We examined her clever little drawings of trees with falling leaves posted on the bulletin board, and we explored her cute little desk in the front row, and we told her how wonderful we thought each and every one of her little accomplishments were.

When our second-born began his trip along the trail of academe, we were pleased to go to his first open house. We checked out his drawings of trees with falling leaves on the bulletin board, and we walked slowly past his desk, and we said nice things about many of his little accomplishments.

When our third-born hit the road to school, we kept the motor running in the parking lot while we dashed inside for his first open house. We glanced at the drawings of trees with falling leaves on the bulletin board, and we sprinted past his desk, and as we got back into the car, we told him that some of his junk wasn't half bad.

By the time we get to our last-born, the road to education is starting to look like an interstate highway. And when I hear about his first open house coming up, I suggest that we flip a coin to see who gets stuck with it.

"You don't have the proper attitude anymore," claims the woman who promised to love, honor and erase my blackboard.

"It's not that. It's just that I think there should be some sort of statute of limitations on how often a parent has to go to open houses in one lifetime. I wonder how many of those things we've gone to, anyway?"

"Twenty-two," she says. "But who's counting?"

We realize, though, that we both have to go. If I don't go, our five-year-old might grow up to hate his father, doubt his self-worth, turn into a chain-saw murderer and become an anarchist. If she doesn't go, the five-year-old might grow up to hate his mother, doubt his self-worth, turn into a chain-saw murderer and become a Democrat.

On the evening of the open house, we drive to school. When we arrive, the parking lot is filled with cars, most of which have their motors running. The only ones who actually have turned off their ignitions are the younger parents, the ones who are smiling as they walk toward the front entrance. I am not surprised. Custer probably smiled on his first visit to Little Bighorn, too.

Inside, the hall is jammed with parents and kids. A large crowd is gathered around the lost and found box.

"What are we looking for this year? I ask the woman who promised to love, honor and pin my mittens to my sleeves.

"A gold stocking cap, a Dukes of Hazzard lunch box and a pair of rubber boots."

"Rubber boots? How could he have lost his rubber boots already? It's only the middle of October."

"He didn't lose them. His brother lost them two years ago. But I keep hoping."

I work my way up to the lost and found box, where I rummage around for a while. I can't find the stocking cap or the rubber boots, but I do find the Dukes of Hazzard lunch box. Judging by its weight, the lunch still is in it.

"When did he lose this?" I ask.

"Three weeks ago," she says.

"Let's wait until we get outside to open it."

We follow the five-year-old down the hall to his room. The first thing he shows us is his drawing on the bulletin board.

"That's a very nice tree," I tell him.

"It's a giraffe," he says.

"Oh. Well, what are those things falling from the top of him?"

"Unsightly dandruff," he says. We've got to find a way to keep him from watching so many television commercials.

Next he leads us to his desk, which is in the front row, within easy reach of the teacher. All of our kids sat in the front row, within easy reach of the teacher, I notice.

The teacher is sitting at her desk when we walk up.

"Are you his father?" she asks, pointing to the five-year-old.

"Yes, I am," I say.

"That explains a lot," she says.

After five minutes I have seen just about everything there is to see. I suggest that we get going.

"We can't leave yet," says the woman who promised to love, honor and drive the getaway car. "We still have to listen to the school band concert and have cookies and Kool-Aid in the gym and say hello to the principal and see about signing up for PTA.

Reluctantly, I walk toward the gym. The road to education is paved with open houses.

16
Home on the range

More and more fathers are learning to cook.

Many social scientists regard this as a manifestation of the American man's newfound ability to break free from outdated sexist stereotypical roles.

I regard it as self-defense.

Like a lot of husbands, I am married to a woman who considers a kitchen the devil's workshop. So after a dozen years of macaroni and cheese that has been microwaved in the box and frozen dinners that are served with salt, pepper and an ice pick, I decide to become a weekend cook.

Before long I can turn out a fairly decent "poulet à l'estragon," an edible "boeuf Bourguignon" and a reasonable facsimile of "piccata di vitello al limone."

But I have no idea how to broil a hamburger.

Which doesn't matter until the night I come home from work to find four pounds of ground meat defrosting on the counter in the kitchen and my three sons in varying stages of malnutrition in front of the television.

"Isn't dinner ready yet?" demands the 12-year-old. "I haven't eaten since lunch."

"Where's your mother?"

"She's doing volunteer work today. She just called and said she won't be home until about eight. We'll probably starve to death by then."

"Why should we starve to death? I'm perfectly capable of fixing dinner."

"On the other hand, we may not live long enough to starve to death."

"Hey, listen. Just because I'm a man doesn't mean I don't know my way around a kitchen. In case you didn't know it, most of the world's great chefs are men"

"Yeah? Name two."

"Colonel Sanders and Chef Boy-Ar-Dee. Now start setting the table and let me get going."

My first step is to check the cupboard to see what ingredients are on hand to combine with the ground meat. Next I take down a cookbook and thumb through it. After 10 minutes of thumbing, I still have not found a recipe that calls for four pounds of ground meat, a can of green beans, a bag of marshmallows and three boxes of Cocoa Puffs.

It is too late to go to the store and too expensive to go to a restaurant. I'm going to have to turn the ground meat into broiled hamburgers.

I begin shaping the ground meat into patties. The seven-year-old wanders into the kitchen while I am working.

"What are those fat things?" he asks.

"Hamburgers."

"Those aren't hamburgers. Hamburgers are real flat and they come in cardboard boxes with mustard and catsup."

"I'm trying something new: meat-flavored hamburgers."

"They'll never sell," he says, wandering away.

When I am finished shaping the meat into patties, I place them on the broiler rack in the oven. It is at this point that I realize that I have no idea what to do next. The only time I ever have broiled hamburgers was in the backyard, wearing Bermuda shorts and dodging Frisbees.

"Hey," I call to the 12-year-old. "When your mother broils hamburgers, how long does she leave them in?"

"I dunno," he says. "Couple of hours, I guess."

I'll never understand how anyone who eats so much can know so little about food.

I put the broiler rack on the top shelf and turn on the controls. In just a few minutes, the patties are making little cooking sounds and changing from bright red to grayish-tan. A few puffs of smoke dance out of the oven through the partially open door.

When the hamburgers have turned from grayish-tan to crispy brown, I turn off the controls and pull out the tray. That's how I discover that only the tops are crispy brown. The undersides still are hot pink.

I turn them over and slide the tray back into the oven. The meat resumes its cooking noises. Little beads of melted fat jump up and hit the heating element, creating quick sparks. A steady parade of smoke is marching out the oven through the partially open door.

When both sides are crispy brown, I pull the tray out and stick a fork into one of the hamburgers. The inside still is as raw as the day it was born. I flip the burgers again and push the tray back in. By now they are up to their chins in grease. Steady bursts of flame are flaring inside the oven. Thick smoke is billowing through the partially open door. It is like cooking inside Mount St. Helen's.

In the midst of all this, I hear a high, whining sound. It is the smoke detector. In my neighbor's living room.

"All right," I yell to the kids in the living room, "these things are almost done. In one minute I expect you to be sitting at the dining room table."

"Are you kidding?" coughs the 12-year-old. "With all this smoke, it'll take us longer than that to find the dining room."

While they crawl along the floor to the dining room, I open the windows in the kitchen, turn on the exhaust fan over the stove and carry the hamburgers into the dining room.

"Neat," shouts the five-year-old when he sees them. "Dad made us licorice balls for dinner."

That's what I get for trying to be a good father. Next time they're getting plain old "piccata di vitello al limone" and liking it.

Actually, it doesn't make that much difference what I cook, because my kids are not fussy. They will turn their noses up at anything.

So just about the only time it makes sense for me to cook is when we're having company. Like on the Sunday a friend from the office comes over to discuss some work. It is, I realize, the perfect opportunity for me to cook. He is fond of Italian food, and I have several Italian recipes I enjoy preparing.

I settle on a meal that features manicotti with Italian sausage as the entree.

"What would go well with my manicotti?" I ask the woman who promised to love, honor and plan my menu.

"Pepto Bismol," she answers.

I plan the meal by myself. To start, there will be Antipasto di Funghi Crudi. Then zuppa con pesto. Followed by the manicotti accompanied by Insalata di Faioli e Tonno and zucchini Parmesan. Except for the manicotti, I have never actually tried any of those things before. But I am sure I will be able to make them. Unfortunately, I will not be able to pronounce them.

On Saturday I go to the store. By the time I have finished buying everything I need for the dinner, I have enough food in my cart to feed the Italian army. By the time I finish paying for it all, I have spent enough money to equip the Italian army.

On Sunday afternoon I point out to the woman who promised to love, honor and respect my space that preparing all of these things is going to require a great deal of concentration and that it would be best if there were a minimum of familial interruptions during the time frame stipulated for these culinary activities.

"What does that mean?" she asks.

"Make sure the kids don't bug me."

She makes sure the kids don't bug me. By taking them to the nearest shopping center. With a purse full of credit cards. By the time this whole thing is over, I suspect, we could have had a cheaper Italian dinner by flying to Naples.

I put the soup on to simmer. While the soup is simmering, I begin to stuff the manicotti. Stuffing manicotti is not nearly as much fun as it might sound. What you have to do is take cylinders of cooked pasta and fill them with a mixture of ricotta cheese, eggs, spices and mozzarella. The whole process is something like putting toothpaste back into the tube. Spoons are too large. Forks are too sharp. Only fingers work well.

I sink my hands into the gooey cheese mixture. I pick up a manicotti shell. The phone rings.

"Somebody get the phone," I yell.

Suddenly I remember that there is nobody else at home. They all are at the shopping center transferring the remainder of our checking account to area merchants. The only ones at home are the dog and I. I glance at the dog. She gives me her it's-probably-not-for-me-anyway look.

I wipe the gooey cheese mixture off of my hands. I dry my hands. I pick up the phone. Whoever it was has hung up.

I hang up the phone and return to the goo. I have stuffed three manicotti shells and am up to biceps in ricotta when the soup that was simmering starts to ooze over the top of the pot, onto the burners and across the stove.

There is no time to wipe off the ricotta cheese. I grab the pot and move it off the burner. Whatever else it is, ricotta cheese does not make good pot holders. I drop the pot, and a lot of the soup splashes out.

I clean up the stove and return to my manicotti stuffing. All these delays have put me behind schedule. My friend is supposed to be here in 20 minutes. According to the directions, the manicotti should cook at 350 degrees for 40 minutes. To get it all done in time, I will have to set the oven at 700 degrees.

At 5 o'clock my family returns and my friend arrives. While we wait for the manicotti, we nibble on antipasto and drink vodka martinis.

When the manicotti is done, I take it out of the oven and put in the zucchini Parmesan to broil. While we wait for it to broil, we drink more vodka martinis.

When the zucchini Parmesan bursts into flame, I take it out of the oven and throw it into the garbage. While we wait for the smoke to clear out of the kitchen, we drink another vodka martini.

Despite my best efforts, dinner will not be exactly as planned. Half the soup is stuck to the top of the stove. Half the manicotti is stuck to the bottom of the baking dish. All of the zucchini is smoldering in the garbage.

If my friend is bothered by all of this, however, he doesn't give any indication. He seems perfectly content as he works on his fourth vodka martini.

It's such a pleasure to cook for someone who really appreciates it.

A lot of my early cooking problems can be blamed on a lack of proper utensils, though. Which I don't realize until I notice the black specks in my food.

I am eating breakfast when I see them for the first time.

"There are black specks in my food," I mention to the woman who promised to love, honor and dish out more than I could take.

"Are they moving?" she asks.

"No."

"It's probably pepper."

"In my oatmeal?"

"Well, maybe not."

That evening at dinner I see them again.

"What did they do, have a special on black specks at the grocery store?" I ask. "They're all over my macaroni and cheese."

"I don't know what they are," she admits. "But, if they taste bad, just pick them out of the macaroni and cheese and throw them away."

"Actually, they don't taste all that bad. In fact, I was thinking of picking them out and throwing the macaroni and cheese away."

"If they don't taste bad, what are you complaining about?"

"I'm not complaining. I'm just curious. I mean, I've gone through a number of cookbooks in the past few years, and I've never noticed any recipes that call for a tablespoon of black specks."

The black specks, we eventually discover, are coming from the pans she bought on sale a few years back. They are green aluminum pans with a black, nonstick surface. Food does not stick to the black surface. But the black surface, unfortunately, is no longer sticking to the green aluminum pans. With each use, a little more of it is flaking off, like black dandruff.

"I think we'd better replace those pans," I point out. "In fact, we could use a bunch of new pans. I was looking through the cupboards and we don't even have a roasting pan big enough to hold a 10-pound roast."

"With the salary you bring home, 10-pound beef roasts are the least of my worries," she says.

The next day I visit a cooking equipment store.

"I want to buy some pans," I tell the clerk.

"What kind?" she asks.

"For cooking."

"Yes, of course. What I meant was, what kind of material were you looking for?"

"What kind is there?"

"The very best are made of copper."

"OK, then, let me have a bunch of those. I've started doing some cooking on weekends, and it doesn't make any sense not to get the full enjoyment out of my leisure time by using anything less than the best equipment."

"You're absolutely right," she agrees. "Now, here's a rather nice French copper roasting pan lined with tin. You'll notice that it has solid brass handles."

"Sounds great. Go ahead and wrap it up. I'm sure it will be a worthwhile investment that will go a long way toward improving the flavor of our food and increasing the dining tastes of my impressionable young children. By the way, how much is it?"

"This one is $315."

"Then again, increase their dining tastes too much and we'll never be able to get the little finks back to Taco Bell."

"You might prefer this nice seven-quart casserole made of extra-heavy-gauge copper with hand-blocked tin lining and riveted brass handles."

"Yes, I might. What does it cost?"

"That price is $250."

"On the other hand, I might not."

"Perhaps this three-piece Calphalon starter set of extra-heavy aluminum with tinned cast-iron handles?"

"How much?"

"$125."

"Not a chance."

"Could I interest you in a 22-piece Tupperware set with styrofoam handles for $7.95?"

I wind up buying two professional-style pans made of an alloy of aluminum, magnesium and silicone with aluminum alloy handles for $90.

The first time I use them I make a Bavarian pot roast in one pan and German green potato soup in the other. When I stir the soup, the spoon scraping across the surface of the aluminum-magnesium-silicone pan sounds like a fingernail running down a blackboard. When I touch the aluminum alloy handle on the pan containing the pot roast, I get a second-degree burn across the palm of my hand.

Worse, the food doesn't really taste any better.

Maybe if I had added a spoonful of black specks.

I don't have much better luck with my turkey-bone soup.

If our weekly grocery bill didn't bear such a strong resemblance to the defense budget, I probably wouldn't even have tried to make turkey-bone soup. But when I see the woman who promised to love, honor and cook my gizzard getting ready to toss out the Christmas turkey carcass, I just have to say something.

"You're not going to throw out those turkey remains, are you?" I ask.

"Of course not," she says. "I'm just putting them in this garbage bag until the hearse gets here from Arlington National Cemetery. I've already arranged for Billy Graham to deliver the eulogy and the Mormon Tabernacle Choir has agreed to fly in and . . ."

"Hey, I'm serious. Considering the price of food, it seems like an awful waste to be throwing any away."

"You're absolutely right," she agrees. "We'll make sandwiches out of what's left. Which do you prefer, mustard or mayonnaise with your turkey-bone sandwiches?"

"Maybe there's not enough there for sandwiches, but there's probably enough for some soup."

"Could be. But who's going to eat it?"

"You mean you don't think the kids would enjoy some nice, hot turkey soup on a cold winter evening?"

"They weren't all that crazy about the turkey the first time around. If you'll remember, they were the ones who said that the perfect Christmas dinner would be pizza with all the trimmings."

"Well, I can't stand the thought of just throwing away perfectly good food. I'm sure if it's properly prepared, they'll eat it."

"Give it your best shot," she says, handing me a dried wingtip on her way out of the kitchen.

The kitchen is all mine. Not to mention the turkey bones. I have never made turkey-bone soup before, but how hard can it be? You put in some bones, add some water, turn on the heat and wait for it to be soup.

I search through the cupboard for a pot big enough to hold the bones left over from an 18-pound turkey. The only thing I can find is a canning kettle, which is just right for holding the turkey, the turkey's wife, all their children and enough water to sink the *Bismarck*.

I toss the bones into the pot and fill it with water. By the time it is full, the turkey is in water deep enough to give Jacques Cousteau the bends, and the kettle is too heavy to lift onto the stove. I pour out some water and hoist it onto a back burner.

While the water heats, I consider what else to add. Vegetables would be good. The trick is finding vegetables they all will eat. The five-year-old hates carrots. The eight-year-old hates onions. The 12-year-old hates celery. The 15-year-old hates corn. The only vegetable upon which they agree is peas. They all hate peas.

I skip the vegetables and throw in a bunch of spices. They don't hate spices. But only because they can't see them.

When the water is boiling, I add some dumplings and turn the heat down to simmer. By early afternoon the soup is done. All I have to do now is remove the bones and I will have enough soup to feed India.

I wait for the soup to cool and then begin to separate the meat from the bones. It is a tedious job, with the monotony broken only by the knowledge that as soon as both of my hands are completely coated with greasy turkey broth, the back of my neck will start to itch.

A few nights later I serve the soup, hot and steaming.

"Boy, this smells good," says the seven-year-old. "What is it?"

"Soup."

"I didn't see any cans."

"It didn't come from a can. I made it myself."

"From what?"

"Oh, water and dumplings and spices and, uh, stuff."

He pokes around in his bowl with his spoon. Under a large dumpling he spots a tiny piece of turkey."

"It's turkey," he cries. "It's LEFTOVER turkey."

Four spoons clatter into their bowls. Four pairs of eyes fix me with accusing stares.

"All right," I confess, "it's turkey leftover from Christmas. But it's really good soup. Honest. It's almost as good as Campbell's."

The rest of the meal is finished quietly and quickly. Then they disappear from the table. They have broken the four-minute dinner. Not one dumpling remains in a bowl. Not one piece of turkey is missing.

"I don't think they loved it," I admit to the woman who promised to love, honor and lick my platter clean.

"Look at it this way," she says. "All you have to do is throw the meat back into the pot, make some more dumplings and you'll have another money-saving meal."

I think I've invented the perpetual turkey.

17
Fathers aren't forever

Not all of the evidence is in yet, but after one girl and three boys, I have come to the conclusion that there are certain differences between them.

A girl will sit for two hours talking on the telephone to a friend who lives on the next block. A boy doesn't necessarily need a telephone to make himself heard on the next block.

A boy will leave his clothes lying all over his bedroom floor. A girl will leave her mother's clothes lying all over her bedroom floor.

A girl will open a can of soup, warm it, take three or four bites and put the rest in the refrigerator. A boy will open three cans of soup, mix them all together, spill half on the floor and leave the rest to harden in a pan on top of the stove.

A boy will be angry with you after an argument at least until dinner time. A girl will be angry with you after an argument until the next time she and her girlfriends need a ride to the roller skating rink.

A little girl will take two dozen Lincoln Logs and build a house. A little boy will take two dozen Lincoln Logs and build a fort.

A girl will spend two hours in the tub, and when she emerges the towels will be wet, the bathmat will be soaked, the water heater will be stone cold and the steam on the mirror over the sink will be an inch and a half deep. A boy will spend two hours in the tub, and when he emerges there will be an inch and a half of water on the floor and the soap still will be dry.

A girl will take her little brothers to the Saturday matinee and come home without their jackets. A boy will take his little brothers to the Saturday matinee and come home without his little brothers.

A girl will put on her best dress to go out for dinner and spill something on it during the meal. A boy will put on his only suit to go out for dinner and spill something on it on the way to the restaurant.

A girl will take a two-pound bag of potato chips to her room and eat them all in one night. A boy will eat a two-pound bag of potato chips in the car on the way home from the store.

A girl will rip the cuff of her oldest Levi's while riding her bike and complain about it until you buy her a new pair. A boy will tear the leg off of his newest school pants playing football in the playground during lunch and not notice.

A girl will take every occasional pillow in the house and arrange them on her bed. A boy will take every occasional pillow in the house and reenact the Civil War in the living room with his brothers.

A girl will answer the phone in the kitchen, yell for you to pick it up in the family room and forget to hang up the extension. A boy will answer the phone in the kitchen and forget to yell for you to pick it up.

A girl will write secret letters to her best friend that no one else can read. A boy will write book reports for English that he can't read.

The one thing they do have in common is that they both grow up to be teenagers.

The trouble with teenagers is that they are at that in-between age. Too old for spanking. But too young for a firing squad.

Despite our best efforts, however, our daughter becomes a teenager. And things begin to change. The food bill goes down, but the Avon lady is bringing eye shadow to our house once a week. In a wheelbarrow. Teenage boys on bicycles go past our house so often that I begin to suspect that they have re-routed the Tour de France.

And my life becomes an eternal busy signal.

"What the heck is going on?" I demand of the woman who promised to love, honor and put me on hold. "Do you realize that I haven't been able to call home from work for the past 42 consecutive days because it is always busy?"

"Really?" she says. "You ought to call the Guinness people. That may be a record."

"How am I going to get to the phone?"

"Well, don't blame me. It's the 15-year-old. The minute she gets home from school she gets on the phone. And there's not a thing I can do to get her off."

"What do you mean there's not a thing you can do? Just tell her to stay off the phone. It's that simple. It's time she understood exactly who is running this house."

"Perhaps you'd like to explain that to her?"

"You're darned right I would. Where is she?"

"On the phone."

Three hours later I catch her between calls and I lay down the law. It is not a pretty scene. There is shouting and yelling, followed by threats and insults and then, of course, the inevitable tears. But, finally, the issue is settled.

"Everything all worked out?" asks the woman who promised to love, honor and put me on hold when I come back downstairs.

"Of course."

"Good. Want to dry your eyes and tell me about it?"

"She's not going to use our phone anymore."

"Really?"

"Really. From now on, she's going to use her own phone."

"What do you mean, her own phone?"

"The one that I'm going to buy for her."

The next day I call the business office of our local telephone monopoly.

"I'd like to have some information about buying a phone," I say.

"That information is available at the Phone Center," the lady on the other end of the line says.

"Good. What's the phone number of the Phone Center?"

"That information is for walk-in customers only," she says. "You can't phone them."

"You can't phone the Phone Center?"

"That is correct."

Still dazzled by the thought that you cannot phone the Phone Center, I drive downtown the next day to where it is located. A blonde woman at the reception desk looks up when I walk in.

"Help you?" she snarls.

It never fails. The more a company spends to advertise how wonderful and friendly it is, the greater the probability that the person it hires to greet its customers will have the personality and charm of a pit bulldog. They call it Ma Bell's Law.

"Well," I say, "I was sort of hoping to buy something from the company that provides your paycheck. But, if I caught you at an inconvenient time, I guess I could come back tomorrow."

"What do you want to buy?"

"How about a nice three-piece suit, maybe in blue, with a contrasting vest and . . ."

"We don't sell clothes here. This is a telephone company."

"OK, you've talked me into it. I'll buy one of those instead."

The Ayatollah's sister takes my name and thumbs me to a seat in the waiting room, where I sit and wait. Eventually my name is called and I report to a woman who is standing behind a counter. Unlike the receptionist, this one did not suck a dozen lemons for lunch.

"Exactly what kind of phone did you wish to buy?" she asks.

"One that's good for about 50 million words."

"Oh, I see, it's for a teenage girl." She shows me the various models of phones.

"I didn't know there were so many different kinds," I admit. "It's going to be tough to make a choice."

"Maybe it would help if you told me what kind of furniture she has in her room," the lady says.

"Well, we bought her this white Early American bedroom set with a real nice canopy bed and all sorts of frilly things around the bottom."

"Our Antique Gold model would go perfectly with that."

"Well, yeah, but last summer she took the bed apart and stuck it in the back of her closet so she could put her mattress on the floor. And now she's got these geometric designs painted on her walls and there's a bunch of stuff hanging from the ceiling, and I'm not really sure if there's any other furniture in there because it is sort of hard to see with all that incense she's always burning."

"Sounds like the Sculptura model would be just right." She shows me the Sculptura model. It is round. Like a toilet seat.

I pay $102 to get the 15-year-old a telephone that looks like a toilet seat, and a few days later a man comes out to hook it up in her bedroom, and 20 seconds later it starts ringing and she runs up to her room to answer it. We do not see her again for three months.

We know she's still living with us, because every morning when we get up there is a quart of ice cream missing from the freezer and a trail of Oreo cookie crumbs leading directly to her door. One night I decide to stay up, just to get a glimpse of her, but around midnight I doze off.

So it comes as quite a surprise when she walks into the family room one evening accompanied by one of her girlfriends.

"I don't suppose you'd drive us over to L'il Sheba's?" she says, fixing me with a look that says if I don't drive her to L'il Sheba's within the next half hour her life will be ruined forever and she might as well shave off all her hair and become a hermit.

"Who the heck is L'il Sheba?" I ask. "And where does she live?"

"L'il Sheba isn't a who," she says. "It's an it. It's a teenage disco that only kids between 13 and 18 can go to. It's in the Forest Park Shopping Center and that's too far to walk."

"Forest Park Shopping Center? That's too far to fly. Can't you find someone else to take you?"

"Well, maybe Bruce could take us?"

"Bruce?"

"He's this guy I met in school. He's got a real neat car that will go from zero to 60 in seven seconds and he finally got his license last week. On the third try."

As I am driving the 15-year-old and her girlfriend to L'il Sheba's, a question occurs to me: How can they be sure that they're admitting only kids between the ages of 13 and 18? I mean, you can prove that you're over 18 by showing your driver's license. But what do you show to prove that you're under 18? Your library card?

The question still is unanswered 45 minutes later when we pull up in front of L'il Sheba's. The 15-year-old and her girlfriend hop out.

"Thanks for the ride, Dad. We'll see you in a couple of hours."

"You'll see me sooner than that. I'm coming in to check this place out."

"Dad," she wails, fixing me with a look that says if she is seen walking into a disco with her father she will be socially disgraced and have no choice but to commit hara-kiri on her nail file.

"Hey, I don't want to come in there any more than you want me to come. But I think it is my duty to make sure that this place is all right. Besides, I'll be darned if I'm going to sit in this car for a couple of hours. And it doesn't make sense for me to spend 45 minutes driving home and then have to turn around and come back for you half an hour later."

"All right," she says, "but you're not actually going to walk in with us, are you?"

"I'll give you a five-minute head start."

While I park the car, the 15-year-old and her girlfriend enter L'il Sheba's. A few minutes later, I follow them. Just inside the door I am stopped by a bouncer Muhammad Ali would hate to meet in a dark alley.

"Going somewhere, fella?" he says.

"Well, yes, I thought I'd come in and sit down for a while."

"What for?"

"Oh, uh, I don't know. Just to look around."

"What's the matter, Pops, can't you find dates your own age?" he asks, tensing his biceps until little ripping sounds can be heard coming from underneath his shirt sleeves.

"Oh no, you've got it all wrong," I say, trying to ignore the droplets of sweat forming on my forehead. "I'm following these two girls who came in her . . . that is, they just got out of my car a few minutes ago and . . . what I'm trying to say is that one of them is my daughter."

"Oh yeah?" he says. "Suppose you just prove that."

"Sure, sure. I'll describe her for you. She's tall and she has blonde hair and she's wearing $25 blue jeans that are eight inches longer than her legs and she's got a callous on her right ear in the shape of a telephone and . . ."

"Okay, I believe you."

I walk inside. L'il Sheba's is located in a large room that also serves as a bingo hall. Other than that it doesn't look anything like a church. In the middle of the room there is a spacious dance floor. Hanging above it are colored lights and the obligatory revolving mirror ball. At the end of the dance floor is a stage where the obligatory dee jay and his two assistants sit and play the records. Disco dee jays always have two assistants to help them play records. I think it's a union rule.

When I come in, the record they are playing is "Shake Your Groove Thing." Which is not to be confused with "Shake Your Body Down to the Ground."

Out on the dance floor, I count 13 teenagers shaking their groove things.

Thirteen?

I count again. There are, indeed, 13 of them. Six couples plus one kid on roller skates. Easily the best dancers are a pretty girl in a white dress and a guy in a black shirt with four buttons open to reveal a chest where thick, curly hair may someday grow.

The record ends and the dee jay puts on another. It is "Blame It on the Boogie." Which is not to be confused with "Boogie Wonderland." This time there are 18 kids dancing. Eight of whom are girls. Still the best dancers on the floor are the girl in the white dress and the guy in the black shirt.

The record changes again. It is "Too Hot to Trot." Which is not to be confused with "Hot Number." Neither of which is to be confused with "Hot Jungle Drums." The guy in the black shirt continues to be the best dancer on the floor. It does not seem to bother him that his partner has left to go to the restroom. Perhaps he has not noticed.

For two hours I sit and watch while the kids who become terminally exhausted at the thought of cleaning their rooms dance their groove things down to the ground without a break. Finally it is time for us to leave. As we walk out the door, they are playing "Last Dance." Which is not to be confused with "Night Dancin'." Neither of which is to be confused with "All Night Dancin'."

None of which is to be confused with "I Could Have Danced All Night." Or any other song with a melody.

Even worse than driving 45 minutes to watch people shake their groove things is having them shaken in your own house. Which happens a few months later when the 15-year-old asks me if she can have a little party in our basement.

What we have, you might say, is your basic communication gap. My concept of a little party is eight or 10 kids sitting around the stereo drinking Cokes and eating Doritos. Her idea of a little party is the Attica prison riots.

"How many kids are you planning to invite?" I ask her.

"Well," she says, "I knew you wouldn't let me invite everybody I wanted to. So I've narrowed it down to 50."

"Fifty? You've got to be kidding. Have you been in your basement lately? There's no way you're going to get 50 kids down there."

"There would be if you'll just move a few things out for the party," she insists.

"Like what, the furnace?"

"Of course not. Just the couch and stuff like that. Anyway, not all 50 kids would be here at the same time. A lot of them would be coming later."

"Like who?"

"Oh, the basketball team."

It could be worse, I realize. It could be the football team. So I agree to let her have the party in our basement and I even agree to let her use my new stereo. And for the next six weeks, every time I tell other parents that I have agreed to have a teenage party in my basement, they just laugh and laugh and laugh.

About two weeks before the party, the 15-year-old meets me at the door when I come home from work.

"Great news," she says. "I won't be needing your stereo for my party."

"That is great news," I agree. "But, why won't you?"

"We're going to have live music."

"Don't tell me. When the basketball team comes over it's bringing along the marching band."

"Don't be silly. It's a rock group from school."

"I think I'd rather have the marching band."

At 4:30 on the afternoon of the party the band comes over to set up in our basement. There are three guys in the group, each of whom carries in 800 pounds of electrical equipment.

"What are the hours that they're going to be playing?" I ask the 15-year-old.

"Between about nine and midnight. Why?"

"No particular reason. I just hope nobody else in town is planning on using any electricity during those hours."

At eight o'clock, the first wave of invited guests arrives. At 8:15, the first wave of uninvited guests follows them. I am alerted to their arrival by the woman who promised to love, honor and raise the drawbridge. She tells me that "there are about a hundred guys standing around in front of our house drinking beer and smoking short cigarettes."

Obviously, I point out to her, there are not really a hundred guys out there. But I open the front door and look out anyway. And, of course, I am right. There are not a hundred guys out there. There are two hundred guys out there.

I walk outside to talk with them. I explain to them that they have not actually been invited to this party and that it would bring me no end of happiness and joy if they would quietly, yet quickly, remove themselves from my property. Or words to that effect.

They, in turn, explain to me that they would be absolutely delighted to leave at some future point in time, but at this particular moment they really don't feel that they can honor my request and if that distresses me then they certainly would not mind if I attempted to perform a physically impossible act. In my hat. Or words to that effect.

So I call the cops.

The cops arrive. Attila's children leave. I return to the party. By this time, the band is playing in the basement. I can tell the band is playing in the basement, because the wallpaper is peeling in the living room. And the woman who promised to love, honor and raise the drawbridge is sitting on the floor.

"Why are you sitting on the floor?" I shout to her.

"I'm not sure," she shouts back. "One minute I was sitting on the couch and the next thing I knew the band started playing and I just sort of vibrated off."

For the next 45 minutes we sit in the living room and feel the band playing downstairs. It is a unique sensation for both of us. But then, we missed the San Francisco earthquake.

After a while the band takes a break and the sounds of silence drift up from the basement. The only thing worse than a bunch of teenagers making noise in a dark basement is a bunch of teenagers being quiet in a dark basement. I decide that this might not be a bad time to sort of casually stroll down there. Just to see if anybody needs any more Doritos, or anything.

On the way to the basement I pass the bathroom. I can't help noticing there is a hole in the door the size of a softball. I am pretty sure it didn't come from the factory that way.

"What happened to the bathroom door?" I ask the 15-year-old when I find her in the basement.

"Uh, well, this girl had to get in there and somebody else was taking sort of a long time and she, uh, sort of tapped on it with her foot."

"Sort of tapped on it? Who the heck is this girl, the Incredible Hulk's sister?"

The hole in the bathroom door, it turns out, is just one of a number of accidents that occur during the evening. Someone accidentally takes a chunk out of a coffee table and someone accidentally tears down a string of Christmas lights and someone accidentally drives his car across our front lawn. Three times.

But a structural engineer assures me that the vibration damage to the foundation is only minimal. And the insurance company says it will only raise my rates about 75 percent to cover the vandalism. And we get a low bid of $150 from a hauling firm to take away the trash in the basement.

The only real problem is with the basketball coach. For the next two weeks he keeps bugging me about coming over to poke around in the remains of the basement. Something about looking for his center and two guards.

With the party only a painful memory in my checkbook, the

15-year-old retires once again to her bedroom. I do not see her again until the following May.

"What's the problem?" I ask her on the day she finally emerges, "Did your telephone melt down?"

"No," she says, "I just thought you'd like to know that the junior-senior prom is coming up. Isn't that neat?"

"Just as long as they're not planning on holding it in our basement."

"Of course not. It's at a ballroom."

"That's nice."

"And I'm invited. I'm going with Bruce."

"That's nice."

"We're going to double date with Karen and Eddie."

"That's ni . . . say, why are you telling me all this?"

"I just thought if you knew all the details it would help when you went with me to pick out my prom dress."

"Me? Why me? I don't know anything about prom dresses. Why don't you ask your mother?"

"She's real busy this week. Besides, you have such good taste in clothes."

"Well, I do have the most extensive collection of leisure suits in the office. But I don't know . . ."

"Please, please go with me."

"Oh, all right."

That night I mention to the woman who promised to love, honor and wear my corsage that the 15-year-old has asked me to help her pick out a prom dress.

"I think she really respects my taste in clothes," I explain.

"That could be," she agrees, "Then again, it could have something to do with the fact that I've already told her I'm not going to lay out $75 for her to buy a dress."

"Seventy-five dollars? You're not serious. I didn't pay that much for my last suit."

"You didn't pay that much for your last two suits."

"Well, I'll tell you one thing. If I have to pay $75 for a dress, she'd better get plenty of use out of it."

"Guess again, Daddy Warbucks. A prom dress can only be worn once."

"That's ridiculous. I can't believe that every one of those dresses at the prom will only be worn once."

"Actually, not every one will. Some of them will get passed down."

"Let's do that, then."

"You can try it. But it's going to be a heck of a struggle getting him into it."

A few days later the 15-year-old takes me and my credit cards out to buy her prom dress. When we arrive at the shopping mall we walk into the first dress shop we come to. She shuffles through several dozen dresses before taking one off the rack.

"What do you think?" she asks, holding it up in front of her. It is a white dress, with a V-neckline and a satin sash. Unfortunately, the bottom of the V meets the top of the sash. It is the first prom dress I have ever seen that looks like it was designed by Frederick's of Hollywood.

"I don't like it," I say.

"Why not?"

"It's too, uh, it's too white."

Three more stores fail to produce anything worth even taking off the rack. Finally, in the fifth store, she finds a dress she likes. She takes it off the rack and goes into the dressing room.

A short while later she emerges from the dressing room and walks hesitantly toward me, a small and uncertain smile on her face. The dress is lovely, with lace and ruffles and little buttons up the front. The toes of her white socks peek out from beneath the floor-length hem as she walks.

And she is beautiful.

It is one of those rare and magic moments. One of those fleeting points in time that makes worthwhile all the hours spent on Christmas Eves putting together doll buggies with one part missing and all the noise from pajama parties that last until dawn and all the frustrations of trying to call home and getting only a busy signal.

"Do you like it?" she asks, softly, with a look on her face that says, "Please, please like it."

"I like it."

"Ever since I was a little girl, I've wanted a dress like this," she says.

Ever since she was a little girl?

She says that as if it was so very long ago, a time only dimly recalled.

And for her, I guess it was. She is about to be 16 and there will never be any more doll buggies for me to put together on Christmas Eve, no more pajama parties that will go noisily into the dawn. She has her own phone now.

She is about to be 16 and I wouldn't have missed this moment for anything, because there will not be many more like them for us.

Fathers are not forever, after all.

Of course, I really should have known that. I should have known it the first time I waited for my oldest son's bedtime kiss and instead he waved from across the room and said, "Well, goodnight Dad."

I should have known it the first time my second son asked me if I'd leave the room because he had to change his clothes now.

I should have known it the first time my smallest son, my very last son, raced down to the bus stop on the first day of school and got on the bus, laughing and eager with his friends. And never looked back.

But seeing her this way, in a white dress with lace and ruffles and little buttons up the front, a dress that looks much too much like a wedding gown, it finally becomes terribly clear to me that my days as a father are numbered.

And just when I was getting the hang of it.